Essential Law

Contracts

Self-Teaching Guide

3rd edition

STERLING Education

3   2   1

ISBN-13: 979-8-8855701-7-6

Sterling Education products are available at quantity discounts.

Contact info@sterling–prep.com.

Sterling Education
6 Liberty Square #11
Boston, MA 02109

Customer Satisfaction Guarantee

Your feedback is important because we strive to provide the highest quality prep materials. Email us comments or suggestions.

info@sterling–prep.com

We reply to emails – check your spam folder

Thank you for choosing our book!

STERLING
Education

From the foundations of constitutional law to complex issues of contracts, the *Essential Law Self-Teaching Guide* series is a perfect compendium to help readers understand multifaceted areas of American Law. Created by highly qualified legal professionals with extensive credentials, these books empower readers to expand their understanding of law.

The content is a clearly presented and systematically organized review of legal principles governing various areas of law. It elucidates the concepts of constitutional rights, criminal law, civil procedure, rules of evidence, contracts, torts, real property, family law, estates, wills and trusts, and business associations.

We commend your desire to learn more about the law. The editors sincerely hope that these guides will be a valuable resource for your learning.

Essential Law Self-Teaching Guides

Constitutional Law	Criminal Law & Procedure
Contracts	Civil Procedure
Evidence	Agency, Partnerships, Corporations & LLCs
Real Property	Family Law
Torts	Wills, Trusts & Estates

Visit our Amazon store

Comprehensive Glossary of Legal Terms

Over 2,100 essential legal terms defined and explained. An excellent reference source for law students, practitioners, and readers seeking an understanding of legal vocabulary and its application.

Landmark U.S. Supreme Court Cases: Essential Summaries

Learn important constitutional cases that shaped American law. Understand how the evolving needs of society intersect with the U.S. Constitution. Summaries of seminal Supreme Court cases focused on legal issues, underlying principles, and judicial decisions.

Visit our Amazon store

Everything You Always Wanted to Know About…

Chemistry

American History

Physics

American Law

Cell and Molecular Biology

American Government and Politics

Organismal Biology

Comparative Government and Politics

Psychology

World History

Environmental Science

European History

Human Geography

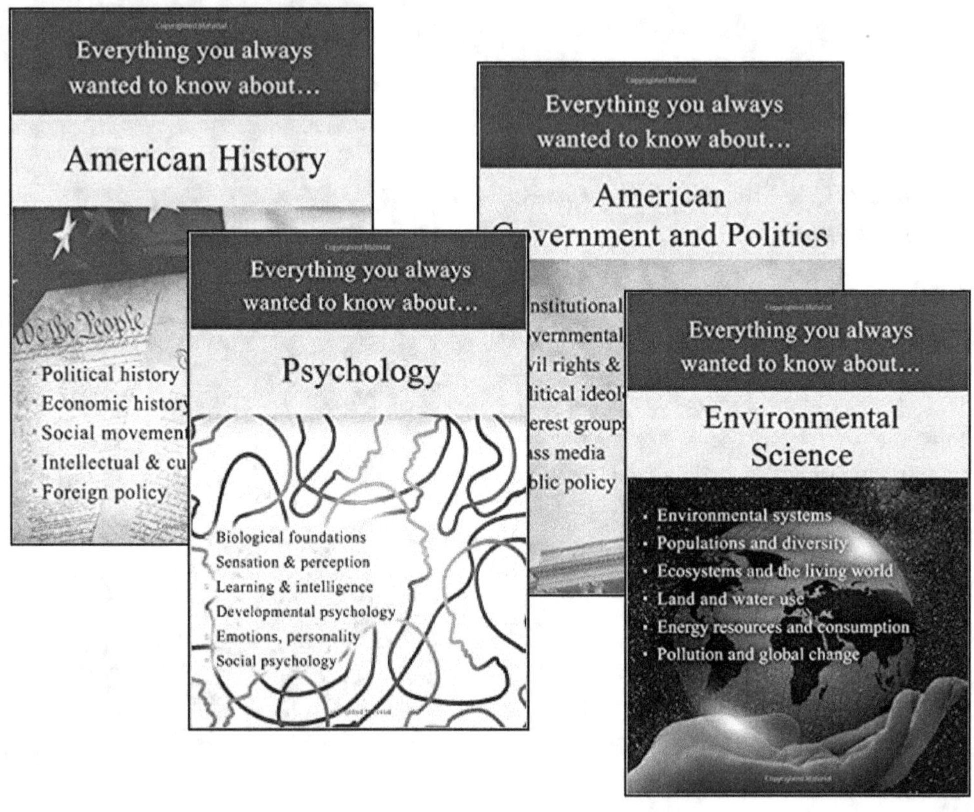

Visit our Amazon store

 Copyright © 2022 Sterling Education.

Table of Contents

GOVERNING LAW (*continued*)

GOVERNING LAW (*continued*)

ANATOMY OF A LAWSUIT (*continued*)

ANATOMY OF A LAWSUIT (*continued*)

APPENDIX (*continued*)

APPENDIX (*continued*)

Constitutional Amendments XI–XXVII (*continued*)

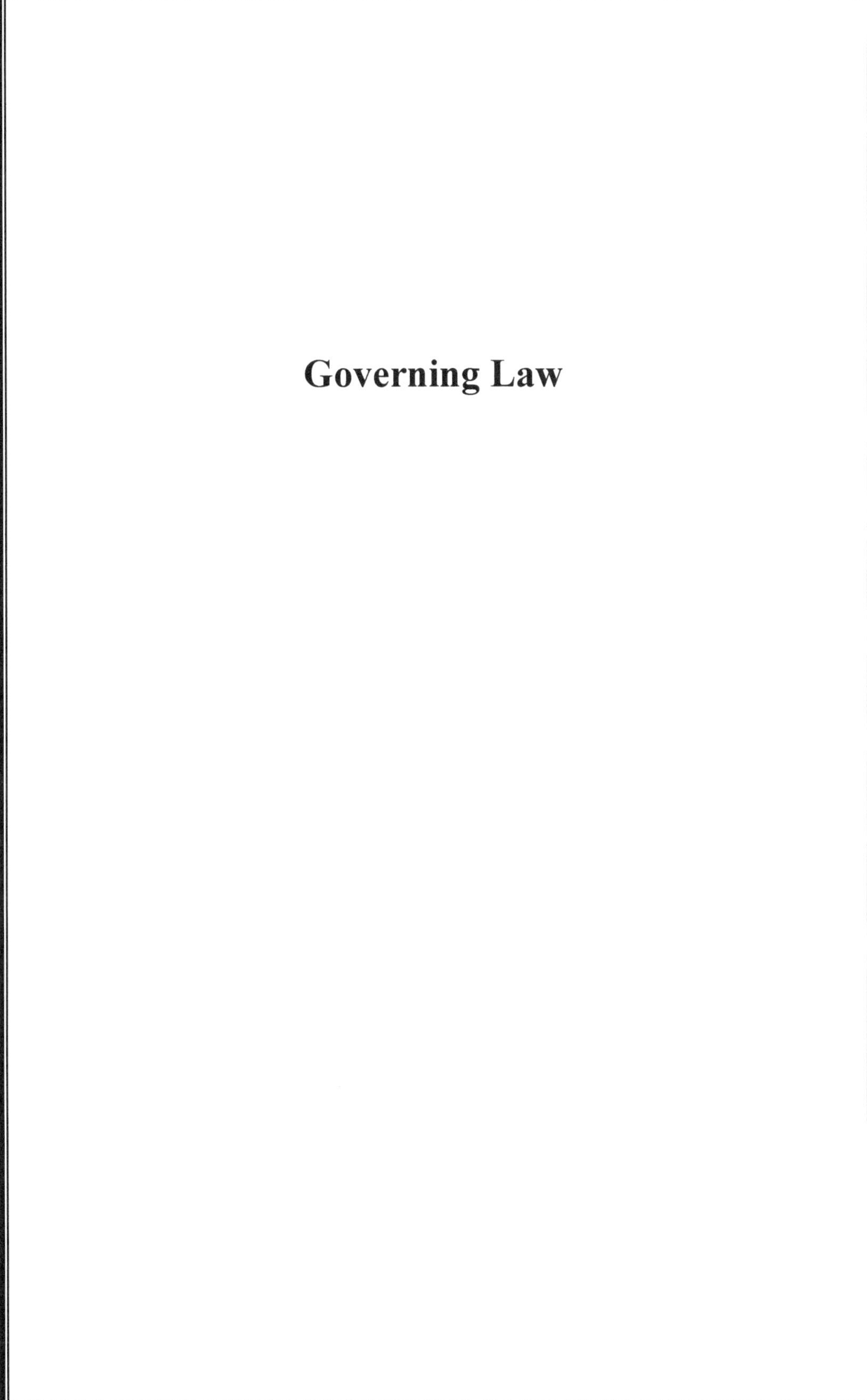

Governing Law

Contract Law – Overview

Definition of and parties to a contract

A *contract* is an agreement that is enforceable by a court of law or equity.

Second Restatement on Contracts: a contract is a promise or a set of promises for the breach of which the law gives a remedy or the performance of which the law recognizes a duty.

Parties to a contract:

> *Offeror* – the party who makes an offer.

> *Offeree* – the party to whom the offer is made.

Requirements of a contract

To be an enforceable contract, the following four basic requirements must be met:

- Agreement – there must be an agreement between the parties.

- Consideration – a *bargained-for* consideration must support the promise.

- Contractual capacity – the parties must have the capacity to contract.

- Lawful object – the object of the contract must be lawful.

Agreement is the manifestation by persons of the contract's substance.

> *Acceptance* is the *manifestation of assent* by the offeree to the terms of the offer.

> Acceptance of the offer creates a contract.

Consideration is the thing of value given in exchange for a promise.

> Gift or gratuitous promises are unenforceable because they lack consideration.

> An *illusory promise* is not enforceable due to a lack of consideration. For example, a promise *to paint a house if time permits*.

Contractual capacity – parties must have mental capacity to be bound by a contract.

Lawful object. The object of the contract must be lawful. A contract to perform an illegal act is void.

> Contracts contrary to public policy are illegal (e.g., murder, theft).

Requirements of the offer

> The offeror must objectively intend to be bound by the offer.

> The terms of the offer must be definite or reasonably certain.

The offer must be communicated to the offeree.

Termination of the offer

A counteroffer simultaneously terminates the offer and creates a new offer.

A contract may be either express or implied.

Express contracts are stated in oral or written words.

Implied-in-fact contracts are implied from the conduct of the parties.

Executed contract has promises made and completed immediately (e.g., product purchase at a store).

Executory contract has promises made but not entirely performed immediately (e.g., apartment lease, painting contract).

Capacity to contract

The law presumes that the parties to a contract have the requisite contractual capacity.

Minors do not always have the maturity, experience, or sophistication needed to enter into contracts with adults.

The infancy doctrine allows minors to disaffirm most contracts with adults.

The minor has the option of choosing whether to enforce the contract.

The contract is voidable by a minor.

Minors are obligated to pay for the necessities of life for which they contract.

Mentally incompetent persons

The law protects people suffering from mental incapacity from enforcing contracts against them.

Intoxicated persons

Most states provide that contracts entered into by intoxicated persons are *voidable* by that person.

The Statute of Frauds – writing requirement

All states have enacted a Statute of Frauds.

Generally, for contracts covered by the Statute of Frauds, an executory contract not in writing is not enforceable.

Contracts must be in writing to be enforceable under the Statute of Frauds (see discussion elsewhere).

Contracts requiring a writing:

1) Land contracts – transfers of ownership interests in real property must be in writing.

2) One-year rule – contracts that cannot be completed within a year (assuming unlimited money and human resources). For example, singing at a person's birthday party in 18 months from contract formation

3) Contracts for the Sales of Goods over $500.

4) Contracts to be responsible as a surety for another's debts.

5) Contracts in consideration of marriage.

6) Contracts by the executor of a will to pay a debt of the estate from their monies.

The formality of the writing requires a signature.

Fraud

Material Misrepresentation of Fact

Intent to deceive

Reliance on the misrepresentation

Injury to the innocent party

Notes for active learning

Formation of Contracts

Offer

To form a contract, there must be an offer that is accepted.

A person makes an "offer" to enter into a bilateral contract by communicating to another person a proposed exchange of promises between the parties. The recipient of the communication reasonably believes that they can enter into a binding contract by accepting that proposed exchange of promises.

The more precise the communication, the more likely it will be characterized as an offer.

Communication is an offer for a unilateral contract if it sets forth valid consideration in exchange for a proposed action by the addressee, in such a manner that the person to whom it is directed reasonably believes that they can enter into a binding contract by performing the requested action.

UCC rule: A sale of goods contract may be made in a manner sufficient to show agreement even though the moment of its making is undetermined.

Acceptance

While rules govern how an offer is accepted in the absence of specific conditions of acceptance set forth in the offer, the offeror has a right to specify the manner of acceptance and make the usual rules inoperative.

If the offeror does not specify conditions for acceptance, an offer may be accepted at a reasonable time and in a reasonable manner.

If the offer is one for a unilateral contract, it may be accepted only by the performance of the act requested, not by a return promise.

Unless the parties have had a course of dealing where the offeree has accepted offers from the offeror by doing nothing, an offeror will be unsuccessful in arguing that silence by the offeree constitutes acceptance.

Unless the terms of an offer or course of dealing permit the offeree to accept by doing nothing, an offeree will be unsuccessful in arguing that they accepted an offer by silence.

For contracts controlled by common law and not the UCC (i.e., common law contracts), the offeree can only accept an offer by communicating acceptance of the terms of the offer before the time the offer expires, is terminated, or revoked.

Unless the offeror requires a different acceptance method in the offer, an offer is accepted when the letter of acceptance is mailed.

Words of the offeree which the offeror can reasonably believe an acceptance will cause a contract to be formed, even if those words do not include the term "accept."

UCC rules: Under § 2-206, an offer to buy goods for prompt shipment is accepted when the seller ships the goods, and a binding contract is formed at that time.

Unless otherwise unambiguously indicated by the language or circumstances,

(a)   an offer to make a contract shall be construed as inviting acceptance in any manner and by any medium reasonable in the circumstances, and,

(b)   an order or another offer to buy goods for prompt or current shipment shall be construed as inviting acceptance, either by a prompt promise to ship or by the prompt or current shipment of conforming or non-conforming goods.

Such a shipment of non-conforming goods does not constitute an acceptance if the seller reasonably notifies the buyer that the shipment is offered only as an accommodation.

Where the beginning of a requested performance is a reasonable mode of acceptance, an offeror who is not notified of acceptance within a reasonable time may treat the offer as having lapsed before acceptance.

UCC rules: Under § 2-207(1), a definite and reasonable expression of acceptance or a written confirmation sent within a reasonable time operates as an acceptance even though it states terms additional to or different from those offered or agreed upon unless acceptance is expressly made conditional on assent to the additional or different terms.

Under § 2-207(2), the additional terms are to be construed as proposals for an addition to the contract.

Between merchants, such terms become part of the contract unless:

(a)   the offer expressly limits acceptance to the terms of the offer,

(b)   the additional terms materially alter the offer, or

(c)   notification of objection to the terms is given within a reasonable time after notice of them is received.

If the proposed additional term materially changes the original offer, there is still a contract, but the additional term is not included.

Under § 2-207(3), conduct by both parties, which recognizes the existence of a contract is sufficient to establish a contract for sale. The writings of the parties do not otherwise establish a contract.

The terms of the contract consist of those terms on which the writings of the parties agree, with supplementary terms incorporated under any other provisions of this Act.

If a seller under the UCC ships non-conforming goods in response to an offer and indicates that they have not accepted the original offer, the shipment of the non-conforming goods is a counteroffer. The seller is not in breach of contract for shipping the non-conforming goods.

If the buyer accepts the non-conforming goods and the counteroffer, they must pay the full contract price.

Revocation of offers

At common law, an offer is revocable by the offeror at any time, even if the offeror promises to keep the offer open for some time.

At common law, an offer is irrevocable if the agreement to keep it open for a specified period is supported by consideration.

Such an offer is an option contract.

The offeror may not revoke an offer for a unilateral contract if the offeror knows that the offeree has commenced substantial performance.

To be effective, the revocation must be communicated to the offeree before the offeree accepts the offer.

A revocation need not be in the express language.

Any communication, such as "I have sold it to someone else," which reasonably indicates to the offeree that the offer has been withdrawn, is a revocation.

A revocation need not be a direct communication between the offeror and the offeree.

If the offeree learns from a third party that the offer has been revoked before the offeree has accepted the offer, the revocation is effective.

An offer for a unilateral contract which occurs when the owner of real estate hires a broker and agrees to pay a commission when and if the broker finds a buyer ready, willing, and able to purchase the property, is automatically revoked without notice if the owner accepts another offer to purchase the property.

A written offer required by the Statute of Frauds can be revoked orally.

The death of the offeror terminates an offer.

If a contract has been formed, either party's death does not terminate the contract unless a party's death makes the contract impossible to perform.

UCC rules: A "merchant" means a person who deals in goods of the kind, or otherwise by their occupation holds themself out as having knowledge or skill peculiar to the practices or goods involved in the transaction, or to whom such knowledge or skill may be attributed by their employment of an agent, broker, or another intermediary who by occupation holds themself out as having knowledge or skill.

"Between merchants" means a transaction for which both parties are chargeable with the knowledge or skill of merchants.

An offer by a merchant to buy or sell goods in a signed writing, which by its terms gives assurances that it will be held open, is not revocable, for lack of consideration, during the time stated, or, if no time is stated, for a reasonable time.

In no event may such period of irrevocability exceed three months.

The offeror must separately sign a term of assurance on a form supplied by the offeree.

An offer by a non-merchant for the sale of goods under the UCC is revocable in the same manner as an offer at common law.

An oral offer by a merchant for the sale of goods is revocable in the same manner as an offer at common law.

A merchant's written offer, which states that the offer remains open for more than three months, remains irrevocable for three months.

Rejection

If at common law, the offeree purports to accept an offer but changes the terms of the offer in any way, the communication is a counteroffer, and no contract is formed.

This rule is qualified for the sale of goods by § 2-207 discussed above.

An offer is terminated by rejection or by a counteroffer. After that, the offeree cannot accept the original offer even if the time to remain open has not expired.

If the offeror has made a multipart offer that can be accepted in part, such as "I will sell you any one of these five lots for $5,000 apiece," acceptance of part of the offer can be considered as a rejection of the remainder of the offer.

An inquiry concerning the offer by the offeree about the offeror's precise terms or willingness of the offeror to modify the terms of the offer is not a rejection.

Mistake, fraud and duress

The defense of unilateral mistake is available when one party's mistake was so apparent that the other party should have known the mistake when the offer was accepted.

Unilateral mistake is grounds for avoiding a contract if the first party is mistaken about a material fact. While not mistaken about that fact, the second party is aware that the first party is mistaken about that material fact.

Mutual mistake is grounds for avoiding a contract if both parties relied on an untrue material fact at the time of contracting.

There is no meeting of the minds, an essential requirement for a contract's existence if each party to the contract without fault has a different understanding of the meaning of the words they agreed to.

If the contract involves the ship "Peerless," but each party innocently and honestly thinks of a different ship named "Peerless," there is no meeting of the minds and no contract.

If the parties orally agree on terms of a contract, which is reduced to writing and the scrivener makes an error in setting out the terms of the contract, either party can reform the written contract to conform to the actual oral understanding of the parties.

Indefiniteness and absence of terms

UCC rule: A contract is not void for indefiniteness if there is no price agreed to. Under UCC, there is a valid contract for a reasonable price.

Capacity to contract

A person who has entered into a contract while a minor can disaffirm that contract, even one that has been completed, except a contract for necessities, within a reasonable time of reaching the age of majority.

If a minor, after reaching majority, agrees to make a payment on a contract they had a right to disaffirm, for an amount which is less than the full contract price, the agreement is only enforceable without new consideration to the extent of the promise made after reaching majority, not for the full contract price.

Implied-in-fact contracts

An implied-in-fact contract arises out of the conscious action of a party.

Without words spoken or written, a contractual obligation can be implied from a party's action. For example, accepting services from someone in providing those services creates an obligation to pay those services' fair value.

If a landowner watches another party perform work on their land, which they know is not intended to be gratuitous and says nothing, the landowner has entered into an implied-in-fact contract to pay for the fair value of the work.

Implied-in-law contracts

An implied-in-law contract arises even though a party has not acted in word or deed to incur contractual liability.

The law will imply a contractual liability to pay for necessary services rendered to an individual when they lack the mental capacity to request such services or agree to be contractually bound to pay.

Quasi-contracts

If parties entered or attempted to enter into a contractual relationship, but the contract is not enforceable because of the Statute of Frauds or other reasons, and one party conferred a benefit on the other, the party conferring the benefit can sue in quasi-contract for the fair value of the benefit conferred. Contract measures of damages do not apply.

A person who has a right to pursue a remedy under an enforceable contract does not have the right to sue in *quantum meruit* (i.e., a reasonable sum of money) for a benefit conferred.

Pre-contractual liability based upon detrimental reliance

If the owner of property puts a construction contract out to bid to general contractors, and a subcontractor submits an offer to perform a subcontract for the general contractor, with the knowledge that the general contractor is relying on the bid when bidding for the general contract, the subcontract's bid is treated as an option contract.

The general contractor's detrimental reliance is a sufficient substitute for bargained-for consideration so that the subcontractor cannot revoke their bid. The general contractor has a reasonable time after they become the successful bidder to accept the bid.

However, since the subcontractor's bid is an offer, there is no contract between the general contractor and the subcontractor until the general contractor accepts the bid.

Unconscionability

Unconscionability arises when there are unfair terms coupled with an unfair bargaining process.

A contract is unconscionable, and a court can refuse to enforce such a contract if one of its provisions was oppressive at the time of the contract's execution.

The concept of unconscionable is part of the UCC and applied with increasing frequency to common law contracts.

Notes for active learning

Consideration

Bargain and exchange

The concept of the bargain is the essence of consideration.

A promise by one party to perform an act or refrain from acting, in exchange for a counter-promise by the other party to perform an act or refrain from acting, constitutes valid consideration, making the promises enforceable.

For valid consideration, the party making the bargain need not be the person benefiting.

An agreement is supported by consideration if the person benefited is a third party for whom the benefit was requested.

If a party promises to do something that they are not legally obligated to, they have given consideration even though the performance of that obligation is not burdensome.

A promise that does not limit a party's rights is an *illusory promise* that does not constitute valid consideration because the promisor possesses a unilateral right to avoid an obligation made in the promise.

"I promise to pay you one dollar for that apple if I choose to" is an illusory promise.

If a promise is illusory because its enforceability is subject to a condition precedent that is entirely within one party's control, a valid contract forms once the condition is satisfied.

The promise to undertake a minor burden imposed on the recipient of property in what is essentially a donative transaction does not transform that burden into consideration.

For example, an aunt's statement to her nephew, "I will buy you a jacket for your birthday if you stop by the store to pick it up," creates a donative transaction because the aunt is not bargaining with her nephew about picking up the jacket.

Adequacy of consideration

In determining whether a contract is supported by consideration, courts do not measure the value of what a party promises compared to what they receive.

An agreement to settle a meritless claim is not valid consideration.

Suppose an agreement is supported by consideration so that a valid contract exists. According to its terms, a party who performs their side of the bargain is entitled to enforce the contract even if they get far more than given.

Detrimental reliance

Even if an agreement is not supported by bargained-for consideration, such as a promise to make a gift, it may be enforceable if there is a substitute for bargained-for consideration; promissory estoppel.

If an agreement is supported by bargained-for consideration, the promissory estoppel elements are irrelevant and the wrong answer to a multiple-choice question.

An agreement not supported by bargained-for consideration, such as a promise to make a gift, is enforceable if promissory estoppel (the substitute for bargained-for consideration) is present.

Promissory estoppel is present if:

1) one party knows that their promise induces substantial reliance by the promisee, and

2) failure to enforce the promise causes substantial hardship, and

3) injustice can be avoided only by such enforcement.

Moral obligations

A service that has already been gratuitously rendered is not valid consideration for a later promise to pay because the bargain element (i.e., the essence of consideration) is absent.

Even though there is no new bargain, a unilateral promise in writing to pay a debt barred by the statute of limitations (SOL) is enforceable without new consideration.

If the new promise differs from the original, the contract is only enforceable to the extent of the new promise.

A contract that was initially voidable because of age is enforceable against that party without new consideration if the minor makes a new promise after reaching majority.

If the new promise differs from the original promise, the contract is only enforceable to the extent of the new promise.

Modification of contracts and pre-existing duty rule

An agreement to rescind an existing executory contract is supported by consideration since each side is bargaining to give up the rights they previously had under the contract.

The common-law rule is that fresh consideration (a different obligation than already agreed to) must support contract modification. The agreement to modify is unenforceable if one party's promises are unmodified and the other party's promises are more burdensome.

A contract can be modified at common law if each gives new consideration for modification.

Consideration is not an issue if one party to an existing contract modifies its promises in exchange for the other party's promise to modify its promises.

Modern common law contract cases hold that an agreement to modify an existing contract without fresh consideration is enforceable when the modification is made in good faith. An example of good faith is when the circumstances under which the contract is to be performed changed through no fault of the parties when the contract was executed.

The traditional common-law rule was that if a party to a contract agreed with the other party to perform an act that they were already obligated to perform because of contractual relations with a third person, the agreement was unenforceable as not supported by consideration.

Under modern contract principles tested, the contractual obligation to a third party to perform the act does not prevent the promise to perform the act from being adequate consideration.

UCC rule: An agreement modifying a contract needs no new consideration to be binding.

Compromise and settlement of claims

Forbearance, a promise not to assert a right, is not valid consideration if the agreement forbears asserting a frivolous claim that the party knows is invalid.

Forbearance is valid consideration if the person seeking to enforce the contract reasonably believes that they have a valid legal claim.

When there is a dispute concerning the amount owed, and one party tenders a check as payment in full, which the other party cashes, there is a discharge of the contractual obligation.

If the claim's amount and validity are undisputed, the cashing of the check does not bar a suit for the remainder.

If there is no dispute concerning either the validity, collectability, or amount of the claim, an agreement to settle the claim for a lower amount is not supported by consideration.

Output and requirements contracts

Output and requirements contracts are not invalid on the grounds of indefiniteness or lack of consideration.

Output and requirements contracts are specifically enforceable if the non-breaching party will have difficulty obtaining substitute performance.

UCC rules: A quantity term expressed as a manufacturer's requirements is enforceable.

UCC § 2-306 provides that "a term which measures the quantity by the . . . requirements of the buyer mean such actual . . . requirements as may occur in good faith . . ."

The definiteness of quantity requirement is satisfied if there is an available objective method for determining the quantity, and the requirements of a manufacturer would generally satisfy that need.

No quantity unreasonably disproportionate to any stated estimate, or in the absence of a stated estimate, to a standard or otherwise comparable prior output or requirements, may be tendered or demanded.

A lawful agreement by either the seller or the buyer for exclusive dealing in the kind of goods concerned imposes, unless otherwise agreed, an obligation by the seller to use best efforts to supply the goods and the buyer to use best efforts to promote their sale.

Third-Party Beneficiary Contracts

Intended beneficiaries

Third-party beneficiary contracts arise when the performance of one of the parties' contractual obligations benefits a person, not a party to the contract, instead of the party who furnished the consideration necessary for that obligation to arise.

Thus "A" and "B" enter into a contract whereby A furnishes consideration to B, who is contractually obligated to render performance to "C," not A.

If two parties contract a service that each intends to benefit a designated third party, the third-party beneficiary and promisee are entitled to sue upon the promisor's breach.

The victim of a breach is entitled to recover only those damages which could not reasonably have been avoided.

Failure to take reasonable steps to mitigate damages defeats a claim for consequential damages.

No contractual rights vest in an intended third-party beneficiary unless the promisor and promisee parties conclude a binding contract.

Third-party beneficiaries are intended beneficiaries when the contracting parties either explicitly or implicitly direct the contract's performance for their benefit.

A *creditor beneficiary* is a type of intended beneficiary where the contract's performance for the benefit of the beneficiary, C, is designed to relieve the party who furnished the consideration, A, from a legal obligation.

A *donee beneficiary* is another type of intended third-party beneficiary where the original contracting party, A, satisfies no legal obligation by entering into a contract designed to benefit C.

Since one of the contracting parties, A, has furnished the consideration which obligated B to perform, the third party, C, need not provide consideration to be able to sue on a third-party beneficiary contract.

A third-party creditor beneficiary, C, does not give up their rights against the contracting party who furnished the consideration, A, which required that performance be rendered to them until the party obligated to render performance, B, completes their obligation.

Intended third-party beneficiaries need not know that a contract has been made for their benefit when they become a third-party beneficiary to have the right to sue.

If a party to a third party beneficiary contract, B, is obligated to render performance to an intended third-party beneficiary, C, in exchange for performance by A., they are relieved of that obligation if A does not perform their obligations to B.

Therefore, B has a valid defense in a suit by C if A fails to perform its obligations to B.

Incidental beneficiaries

An incidental beneficiary, a person benefited if a contract between two other parties is performed but is a person that the original contracting parties did not intend to benefit, has no right to enforce a third-party beneficiary contract.

Modification of the third-party beneficiary's rights

The two original parties to a third-party beneficiary contract, A and B, can modify or rescind their contract to the detriment of the intended beneficiary, C, up until the time that C's rights in the contract become vested.

They become vested when C either assents to the contract at a party's request, sues on the contract, or changes position in reliance on it.

Assignment and Delegation

Assignment of rights

An assignee succeeds in a contract as the contract stands at the time of assignment.

Once a party has fully performed obligations under a contract, their right to return performance, including the right to sue for breach of the other party's obligations, can be assigned to a third party even if the contract prohibits assignment.

A party to a contract can assign the benefits of the contract, which accrue without obligating the assignee to assume the burdens of the contract.

An assignee of a contract only obtains rights under it, which are limited by defenses that the original contracting party has against the assignor.

The rule is contrary to the rule when the assignment is a negotiable instrument.

The assignee, known as a *holder in due course*, takes free of the personal defenses that the other party to the negotiable instrument has against the instrument's assignor.

If a contracting party pays a second contracting party an amount due on the contract before receiving notice that the second party assigned their interest under the contract, the first party is not obligated to an assignee, even though the assignment took place before the payment.

If the first party has been notified of the assignment before making payment, they can only discharge their contract obligation by paying the assignee.

UCC rule: Unless otherwise agreed, all rights of either seller or buyer can be assigned except where the assignment would materially change the duty of the other party, increase materially the burden or risk imposed by contract, or impair their chances of obtaining return performance materially.

Unless the circumstances indicate the contrary, a prohibition of the contract assignment is to be construed as barring only the delegation to the assignee of the assignor's performance.

Delegation of duties

A contractual provision forbidding delegation is valid and enforceable.

A party may perform their duty through a delegatee unless:

1) it is otherwise agreed, or

2) the other party has a substantial interest in having the original promisor perform, or

3) the party wishing to delegate possesses unique characteristics (e.g., a singer), so the performance by a delegatee materially alters the bargained-for performance.

No delegation of performance relieves the party delegating duty to perform or liability for breach.

If the parties enter into a novation so that one original contracting party agrees to look solely to the delegatee for performance in exchange for releasing the other original party from the contract's obligations, the original party is no longer liable if the delegatee breaches the contract.

UCC rule: An assignment of "the contract" or "all my rights under the contract" or an assignment in similarly general terms is an assignment of rights and duties.

Unless the language or the circumstances (e.g., an assignment for security) indicate to the contrary, it is a delegation of the duties of the assignor's performance.

The acceptance of the assignee's assignment constitutes a promise to perform those duties.

The promise is enforceable by the assignor or the other party to the original contract.

Statute of Frauds

The exemption of contracts for less than $500 from the Statute of Frauds requirements applies only to contracts for the sale of goods governed by UCC-2.

Memorandum

The Statute of Frauds applies to specific types of contracts discussed below. The contract itself need not be in writing to satisfy the statute.

There need only be a memorandum that contains the essential terms of the contract signed by the party to be charged.

The memorandum sufficient to satisfy the statute need not be written when making the promise, nor need it to be writing addressed to the promisee.

Contract cannot be performed within one year

In measuring the one year to determine if the Statute of Frauds is applicable, the period starts when making the contract, not at the commencement of performance.

The Statute of Frauds applies to an eleven-month personal services contract made on January 1 with work starting on April 1, since the contract will not terminate until March 1 of the following year.

The possibility that death could prematurely terminate a personal services contract for more than a year does not cause the Statute of Frauds to be inapplicable.

The Statute of Frauds does not apply to a personal services contract for the life of the party because the natural termination of that contract could occur within a year.

Land contracts

See Property Law for the Statute of Frauds as it applies to land contracts.

A real estate brokerage contract is enforceable even if there is no memorandum signed by the property owner sufficient to satisfy the Statute of Frauds.

General rule for the sale of goods

UCC rules: Except as otherwise provided, a contract for the sale of goods for the price of $500 or more is not enforceable by action or defense unless there is a writing sufficient to indicate that a contract for sale had been made between the parties.

This writing must be signed by the party against whom enforcement is sought or by their authorized agent or broker.

A writing is not insufficient because it omits or incorrectly states a term agreed upon, but the contract is not enforceable beyond the number of goods shown in such writing.

A memorandum satisfies the Statute of Frauds if it indicates a contract; it contains a description of the goods, quantity and is signed. It does not need to contain the price.

Exceptions for sale of goods

UCC rules: Between merchants, if within a reasonable time a writing in confirmation of the contract and sufficient against the sender is received, and the party receiving it has reason to know its content, it satisfies the requirement of the Statute of Frauds against such party unless written notice of objection to its contents is given within ten days after it is received.

A contract that does not satisfy the general rule, but which is valid in other respects is enforceable if:

1) the goods are to be specifically manufactured for the buyer and are not suitable for sale to others in the ordinary course of the seller's business, and the seller, before notice of repudiation is received and under circumstances which reasonably indicated that the goods are for the buyer, has made either a substantial beginning of manufacture or commitments for their procurement, or

2) the party against whom enforcement is sought admits in pleadings, testimony, or in court that a contract for sale was made, but the contract is not enforceable under this provision beyond the number of goods admitted, or

3) for goods for which payment has been made or accepted or which have been received or accepted.

If, as modified, a UCC contract involves a sale of goods for more than $500, it requires compliance with the Statute of Frauds.

Suretyship

An oral promise to pay another's debt is usually unenforceable because of the Statute of Frauds.

If the primary purpose of the promise to pay another's debt is to further the promisor's goals, the promise is enforceable even if there is no memorandum signed by the promisor sufficient to satisfy the Statute of Frauds.

In addition to the writing required by the Statute of Frauds, a party seeking to collect from a surety must give reasonable notice to the surety that they have extended credit to the other party to the contract.

The suretyship provisions of the Statute of Frauds are inapplicable unless there is:

1) a contractual relationship between the creditor and the party who is to benefit from the services, and

2) the creditor knows that the defendant is acting in a suretyship capacity rather than in a direct contractual capacity.

Notes for active learning

Parol Evidence Rule

The *parol evidence* rule bars evidence of prior or contemporaneous statements that contradict the terms of a written contract.

If the written contract is integrated, evidence of prior or contemporaneous agreements between the parties is inadmissible.

Exceptions to the parol evidence rule

However, *parol evidence* for the terms of a contract is admissible:

1) to prove that there is a condition precedent to a contract's coming into existence;

2) to explain an ambiguity;

3) to show that the parties used words in a nontraditional manner or spoke in code;

4) to prove a mistake in reducing the terms of an oral agreement to writing;

5) to prove contract modification by evidence of conversations after contract formation.

   At common law, a provision in a written agreement that a writing can only modify a contract is not valid;

6) to prove, for an oral contract which is not integrated, subjects not covered by the written contract.

UCC rules: The terms to which the confirmatory memoranda of the parties agree, or which are set forth in writing intended by the parties as a final expression of their agreement may not be contradicted by evidence of prior or contemporaneous oral agreement but may be explained or supplemented by:

1) *course of dealing, usage of trade,* or *course of performance,* or

2) evidence of consistent additional terms unless the court finds the writing was intended as a complete and exclusive statement of the terms of the agreement.

When inconsistent with usage of trade, a course of dealing trumps usage of trade and controls the interpretation of the contract.

Unlike the rule at common law, under the UCC, a signed agreement that excludes modification or rescission except by a signed writing cannot be modified or rescinded.

Except for between merchants, such a requirement on a form supplied by the merchant must be separately signed by the other party.

Although an attempt at modification or rescission does not satisfy the UCC provisions for the Statute of Frauds or *parol evidence* rule, it can operate as a waiver.

Notes for active learning

Interpretation of Contracts

Employment-at-will

The primary goal in interpreting a contract is to carry out the intent of the parties.

Permanent employment means employment-at-will.

In an employment-at-will relationship, either party can terminate the agreement at any time without termination being a breach unless the termination violates public policy.

> When parties attach significantly different meanings to the same material term, the meaning that controls is that "attached by one of them if at the time the agreement was made . . . that party did not know of any different meaning attached by the other, and the other knew the meaning attached by the first party." Restatement (Second) of Contracts § 201.

UCC course of dealing and usage of trade

UCC rules: A *course of dealing* is a sequence of previous conduct between the parties to a particular transaction, which is reasonably regarded as establishing a common basis of understanding for interpreting their expressions and other conduct.

A *usage of trade* is a practice or method of dealing with such regularity of observance in a place, vocation, or trade to justify an expectation that it will be observed for the transaction in question.

The existence and scope of such usage are to be proved as facts.

If it is established that such a usage is embodied in a written trade code or similar writing, the interpretation of the writing is for the court.

A course of dealing between parties and usage of trade in the vocation or trade in which they are engaged, or of which they are or should be aware, shall give meaning to, and supplement or qualify, terms of an agreement.

The express terms of an agreement and an applicable *course of dealing* or *usage of trade* shall be construed wherever reasonable as consistent with each other.

When such construction is unreasonable, express terms control both the course of dealing and usage of trade, and the course of dealing controls usage of trade.

Notes for active learning

Conditions

Express conditions

If the obligation of one party to a contract to perform under that contract is subject to an express condition precedent, the other party seeking to establish a breach must either show compliance with an express condition or that the other party was in bad faith for the condition, thereby excusing compliance with the condition.

A contract condition that performance be satisfactory to the purchaser means that an objective standard will be applied, and performance must be satisfactory to a reasonable person.

If the contract involves personal taste, the performance must be subjectively satisfactory to the purchaser.

Even when the subjective standard is applied, the purchaser must act in good faith.

If one party assumes an obligation and the size of which at the time of contracting is unknown, they are entitled to be paid the consideration promised, even if the obligation is substantially smaller than anticipated.

If a certificate of completion by the architect is a condition of completing a construction contract, the builder cannot collect in full under the contract until that certificate is obtained unless they prove that the architect failed to provide it because of bad faith.

If it is clear that the purpose of the condition was to benefit or protect one of the parties, that party may waive the condition and insist that the other party perform.

Constructive conditions of exchange

If no order of performance is specified in the contract, each party must perform its obligations under the contract as a condition for demanding performance from the other.

For example, in a sale of goods contract, the buyer must pay for the goods, and the seller must deliver the goods simultaneously. Such mutual conditions precedent is constructive conditions of exchange.

The parties to a contract can make the performance by one party a condition precedent to the performance by the other.

Absent a special provision concerning partial payment in the contract; a party has no right to be paid until they complete the required performance.

If the time for performance is not made of the essence, a party may perform in a reasonable time.

Divisible contracts

A divisible contract occurs when performance by one party of less than the full contractual obligation gives that party a right to require partial performance of the other party's obligation.

For example, if A is employed by B for one year, B will ordinarily have an obligation to pay A a portion of their yearly salary periodically.

If a contract is divisible, one divisible portion's performance permits the plaintiff to demand performance from the defendant for that separable portion, even if the plaintiff is in breach of another separable portion.

For example, if A, the employee on an annual salary with monthly pay periods, works for one month, they are entitled to be paid for that month's work, even if they do not complete the full year's employment.

Contract law acknowledges the fact that parties sometimes embody obligations that are, in most respects, separable into a single document or agreement.

Rules for damages permit the separable parts to be treated separately.

Though the contract has separable components for damages, it is still a single contract permitting the damages suffered by each side to be litigated in a single lawsuit.

If the contract requires one party to perform a single task (e.g., building a structure), the fact that the contract requires periodic payments does not make it a divisible contract.

Immaterial breach and substantial performance

Under the common law, the plaintiff can sue for breach of contract and collect contract damages if they have substantially performed the contract, even if there is an immaterial (non-willful) breach.

If the plaintiff has not fully performed the contract, the defendant can successfully assert a counterclaim for damages caused by the plaintiff's failure to perform fully.

UCC rule: The UCC does not recognize the doctrine of substantial performance. Instead, it follows the rule of *perfect tender*.

Except for an installment contract, the seller must tender the correct amount of conforming goods at the time specified, or the buyer can reject the goods without liability and sue the seller for damages.

Installment contracts

UCC rules: An installment contract is one where the seller does not have an obligation to deliver all the goods to be sold under the contract at one time.

If a contract is determined to be an installment contract, the rule of perfect tender, which permits the buyer to reject non-conforming goods if all goods are to be delivered at one time, is inapplicable.

The buyer can reject a nonconforming shipment only if it substantially impairs the installment value and cannot be cured.

A failure by the seller to deliver the appropriate quantity of conforming goods on time for one installment of an installment contract is a breach of the total contract only if the nonconformity substantially impairs the entire contract's value.

UCC rule – implied warranty of merchantability

All merchant sellers give implied warranties of merchantability.

UCC § 2-314(2) defines the implied warranty of merchantability:

1) goods, to be merchantable, must at least pass without objection in the trade under the contract description; and

2) in the case of fungible goods are of a fair average quality within the description; and

3) are fit for the ordinary purpose for which goods are used; and

4) run within the variations permitted by the agreement, or even kind of quality and quantity within each unit and among all units involved; and

5) are adequately contained, packaged, and labeled as the agreement may require; and

6) conform to promises or affirmations made on the container or label, if any.

UCC rule – warranty of fitness for a particular purpose

Under UCC § 2- 315, a warranty of fitness for a particular purpose arises whenever the seller has reason to know of any particular purpose for which the goods are required. The buyer is relying upon the seller's skill to select suitable goods.

Constructive condition of cooperation

A condition of cooperation is implied in every contract.

A party who wrongfully hinders the other party's performance breaches the contract.

Each party to a contract has an implied duty to cooperate with the other party in achieving the objects of the contract.

Obligations of good faith and fair dealing

Each party to a contract has an implied duty to act in good faith.

Acting in bad faith can constitute a breach of contract and give the other party a defense to a suit for breach of contract.

Suspension or excuse of conditions by waiver

A waiver occurs when a party to a contract affirmatively represents to the other party that it will not act on or enforce a known right.

A waiver is revocable unless the other party relies on the waiver to their detriment, or the waiver is an agreement supported by consideration.

The conduct of a contracting party in failing to insist on full performance for some time can constitute a course of dealings and a waiver of the right to full performance during the remainder of the contract if relied upon by the other party to their detriment.

If the certification of a condition's performance is placed in a third party to benefit one of the contracting parties, that contracting party can waive the certification.

UCC rule: A party who had made a waiver affecting an executory portion of the contract may retract the waiver by notification to the other party so that strict performance of terms waived will be required unless the retraction would be unjust due to a material change of position in reliance on the waiver.

Remedies

Rescission

When a seller induces a buyer's consent to a contract through a material misrepresentation, the resulting contract is voidable at the election of the buyer.

In some cases, a failure to independently inspect property might constitute a defense to a claim of misrepresentation.

The buyer is entitled to rely on the truth of the seller's material representations and need not conduct independent tests to see whether the seller is lying.

Buyer's and seller's obligations unless terms are specified

UCC rule: The seller must tender conforming goods at their place of business at the specified time, and the buyer has a concurrent obligation to pay the purchase price at that time.

Cure

UCC rules: Where tender or delivery by the seller is rejected because it is non-conforming and the time for performance has not yet expired, the seller may timely notify the buyer of the intention to cure and within the contract time make a conforming delivery.

Where the buyer rejects a non-conforming tender which the seller had reasonable grounds to believe to be acceptable with or without money allowance, the seller may, if they seasonably notify the buyer, have a further reasonable time to substitute a conforming tender.

Rights of the non-breaching party

UCC rule: If a party to a contract has committed a material breach, the non-breaching party is excused from further performance of the contract.

Demand for assurances

UCC rule: A contract for the sale of goods imposes an obligation on each party that the other's expectation of receiving due performance will not be impaired.

When reasonable grounds for insecurity arise concerning either party's performance, the other may in writing demand adequate assurance of performance. Until receiving such assurance, if commercially reasonable, the requesting party may suspend performance for which they have not already received the agreed return.

Acceptance of improper delivery or payment does not prejudice the aggrieved party's right to demand adequate future performance assurance.

After receipt of a justified demand, failure to provide within a reasonable time, not exceeding thirty days, such assurance of due performance is adequate under the case's circumstances and is a repudiation of the contract.

Anticipatory repudiation

Anticipatory repudiation occurs when a party to the contract gives unequivocal notice to the other party that they will not perform their obligations at the time set for performance.

If the non-repudiating party has not relied on anticipatory repudiation by canceling the contract or materially changing their position, the repudiating party may retract the repudiation, providing they give adequate assurances.

The non-repudiating party has no right to sue for a breach before the time of scheduled performance.

UCC rule: When either party repudiates the contract concerning a performance not yet due, the loss of which will substantially impair the value of the contract to the other, the aggrieved party may:

1) for a commercially reasonable time await performance by the repudiating party; or

2) resort to a remedy for breach even though they have notified the repudiating party that they would await the latter's performance and has urged retraction; and,

3) in either case, suspend their performance or proceed following this article's provisions on the seller's right to identify goods to the contract notwithstanding the breach or salvage unfinished goods.

Risk of loss

UCC rules: The risk of loss is initially on the seller.

The risk of loss shifts to the buyer when the seller completes delivery obligation for goods that meet the contract's quantity and quality specifications.

If nothing is said about the place of delivery or the contract specifies that delivery is at the seller's place of business, the risk of loss shifts to the buyer when the seller places conforming goods on a common carrier with instructions shipped to the buyer.

If the contract requires delivery at the buyer's place of business, the risk of loss does not shift to the buyer until conforming goods arrive at the buyer's place of business.

If the goods shipped are non-conforming, the seller retains the risk of loss until accepted.

If the buyer initially accepts the goods and rightfully revokes acceptance, the risk of loss is on the buyer only to the extent that the buyer's insurance covers the goods.

Rights of *bona fide* purchasers

UCC rule: A *bona fide* purchaser of goods from a person in the business of selling those goods takes superior title to the true owner of those goods.

Seller's remedies in the event of buyer's breach

UCC rules: The standard measure of damages for non-acceptance or repudiation by the buyer is the difference between the market price at the time and place for tender and the unpaid contract price, together with incidental damages but less expenses saved in consequence of the buyer's breach.

If the measure of damages provided in the preceding paragraph is inadequate to put the seller in as good a position as performance would have done.

The measure of damages is the profit (including reasonable overhead), which the seller would have made from the buyer's full performance, together with incidental damages provided in this article, due allowances for costs reasonably incurred, and due credit for payments or proceeds of resale.

As a limited alternative remedy, the seller may make the goods available to the buyer and sue for the contract price if the goods cannot be sold in the seller's ordinary course of business.

Buyer's remedies in the event of seller's breach

UCC rules: The buyer may seek damages – the difference between the market price and the contract price.

The buyer may fix damages by purchasing the goods elsewhere and collect the difference between the price they pay and the contract price; this remedy is *cover*.

The buyer may tender the full purchase price and seek an order requiring the seller to deliver the goods if they are unique.

Measure of damages

Expectancy damages are the standard measure of contract damages, i.e., the amount of money that would put them in the same position as if the breaching party had performed their obligations under the contract.

The amount of a non-breaching party's expectancy damages on a contract where the non-breaching party has not expended money towards their obligated performance is the profit they would have made had the contract been performed.

If the non-breaching party has expended money in the performance of their obligations under the contract, they are entitled to recover those sums plus profit.

If expectancy damages are too speculative and cannot be recovered, the non-breaching party is entitled to reliance damages, the amount expended to perform the contract, whether or not those expenditures benefited the breaching party.

If payments on a contract are due in installments and there is no acceleration clause, the non-breaching party can only sue for the unpaid installments.

If a party voluntarily incurs additional expenses toward the performance of the contract after they know that the other party is in breach, they may not recover those additional expenses.

A non-breaching party has a duty to mitigate damages by taking steps to avoid damages they should have foreseen and could have avoided without undue risk, expense, or humiliation.

For example, if the employer breaches an employment contract, the employee must use reasonable efforts to seek substitute employment during the remainder of the contract period.

If they fail to mitigate, the fair value of what they would have received if they had found other employment is deducted from their expectancy damages.

If incurred to mitigate damage after the breach, reasonable expenses are recoverable as incidental damages, even if expenses are not connected to a successful mitigation attempt.

The victim of a breach is entitled to recover only those damages which could not reasonably have been avoided.

Failure to take reasonable steps to mitigate damages defeats a claim for consequential damages.

Consequential damages

Consequential damages are limited to those damages that were reasonably foreseeable by the parties when the contract is made.

Liquidated damages

A provision fixing liquidated damages is unenforceable unless the amount fixed is reasonable compared to the damages that the parties could anticipate when making the contract or the damages incurred.

Specific performance

The buyer and seller are entitled to sue for specific performance of enforceable land contracts.

Specific performance requiring the defendant to perform is not available to remedy a personal services contract.

A negative injunction can be granted by the standards for granting injunctions, preventing the defendant from working for a person other than the one to whom contractually bound.

Restitution damages (*quantum meruit*)

If a party is prevented from suing on the contract because the contract is unenforceable (e.g., Statute of Frauds) or because they committed a material breach, they are limited to restitution damages.

Restitution (or *quantum meruit*) damages are the fair value of the benefit conferred on the other party.

An unjust enrichment claim cannot exceed the contract price when all the work giving rise to the claim has been performed, and the only remaining obligation is the payment of the price.

Restitution damages cannot be greater than the recoverable damages if the contract were enforceable.

Notes for active learning

Monetary Damages for Breach of Contract Parties

Monetary damages are of three types: compensatory, consequential, and liquidated.

Compensatory damages are intended to compensate a non-breaching party for the loss of the bargain. They place the non-breaching party in the same position as if the contract has been entirely performed by restoring the "benefit of the bargain." Additionally, a non-breaching party can sometimes recover consequential or special damages from the breaching party.

Consequential damages are foreseeable damages that arise from circumstances outside the contract. To be liable for consequential damages, the breaching party must know or have reason to know that the breach will cause special damages to the other party.

Moreover, under certain circumstances, the parties to a contract may agree in advance to the amount of damages payable upon a breach of contract as *liquidated damages*. To be lawful, the damages must be difficult or impracticable to determine, and the liquidated amount must be reasonable in the circumstances. An enforceable liquidated damage clause is an exclusive remedy even if actual damages are later determined to be different.

A liquidated damages clause is considered a penalty if actual damages are determinable in advance or the liquidated damages are excessive or unconscionable, in which case the liquidated damages clause is unenforceable. The non-breaching party may then seek actual damages.

Notes for active learning

Impossibility and Frustration

Impossibility of performance

If events after the formation of a contract make the performance by one party illegal or impossible, the doctrine of impossibility is applicable, and the parties are discharged from their contractual obligations.

The doctrine of impossibility applies at common law when the contract's subject matter is destroyed, or a party to a personal service contract dies.

The destruction of an existing structure renders a contract to repair it impossible, terminating the contract.

The contractor has the right to collect for the fair value of the work done in *quantum meruit* but cannot sue for contract damages because the contract obligations have been discharged.

A party may not rely on the defense of impossibility if they expressly assume the risk of performing an objectively impossible obligation.

Excused performance under the UCC

UCC rules: Under the doctrine of impracticability, performance is excused when:

1) goods identified to the contract are destroyed,

2) performance becomes illegal,

3) performance is prevented by a non-foreseeable event, the nonoccurrence of a basic assumption of the contract.

Under § 2-615, when a contract specifies produce to be grown on a specific farm and the crop is destroyed by natural forces beyond the farmer's control, the farmer is excused from performance to the extent of the damage.

Notes for active learning

Conflict of Laws in Contracts

Place of contracting

Contracts – *lex loci contractus* (*"law of the place where the contract is made"*) applies.

Issues concerning performance are governed by the law of the place of performance.

The forum decides where the contract was made.

The state whose law is applied to the dispute may have no interests at stake (other than being the place of contracting).

Where the contract is made is subject to interpretation based upon the nature of the modern commercial transaction.

The issue may be characterized as one of performance to apply different laws and achieve the desired result. In *Louis-Dreyfus v. Paterson Steamships, Ltd* (1930), each state favored limiting liability, but the *lex loci* rule did not. To advance the interests of the involved states, the court characterized the dispute as performance.

Contracts – party expectations may determine the choice of law.

A court may ignore the *lex loci* law and apply the law of the place of performance to resolve a contract dispute if it determines that the parties entered into their obligation because of that law (contract is invalid under *lex loci* law but enforceable in place of performance)

An adhesion contract (steamship ticket) may designate the law to be applied regardless of *lex loci* if the forum selected has some connection to the agreement.

Usury – courts tend to apply whichever law upholds the validity of the contract if there is a reasonable relationship to the transaction and the parties were in equal bargaining positions.

2nd Restatement § 203 usury – a contract is enforceable if its interest rate is permitted in a state with a substantial relationship to the contract and does not significantly exceed the price allowed by an interested state.

The presumption of validity is necessary to promote the free flow of commerce; otherwise, lenders may be reluctant to lend money.

Rights under a contract vest at the moment the contract is made.

Clear rules but may lead to a state with no policy interest in the outcome of the litigation.

American rule: the place of contract for specific issues (e.g., validity, capacity).

The place of contract determines capacity.

Special rules

Special rules determine where the contract is made depending on the type of conflict.

§311 Place of contracting: principal event necessary to make a contract occurs.

§312 Formal contract: effective on delivery, place of contracting is where delivery is made.

§323 Informal unilateral contract: where the event takes place that makes it binding.

§325 Informal bilateral contract: where the second promise is made in consideration of the first promise.

§326 Acceptance from one state to another: if acceptance is sent by an agent of the acceptor, the state where the agent delivers it or from which acceptance is sent.

§332 Validity and effect of the contract: the law of the place where the contract was made (capacity, necessary form, consideration, requirements to make a promise binding, time, and place where the promise is to be performed, the character of the promise).

§358: performance handled with the place where a contract is to be performed (i.e., manner, time, locality, parties involved, sufficiency, an excuse for non-performance).

Justifiable expectations of parties are enforceable.

Place of performance for other issues

Old law: the law only if there is a connection.

If a contract is completed in another state, it makes no difference whether the person goes in person, sends an agent, or writes a letter across the boundary lines between the states.

English rule: parties' intent, if unclear, is the "closest and most real connection."

Rome Convention eliminated "mandatory rules," replacing them with "overriding mandatory provisions."

Party autonomy – parties may choose but be limited by "mandatory rules" of the country where the contract was made.

A court can apply its law if it considers the law "overriding," providing much discretion.

Default rule (absent choice) § 4 – "most closely connected."

Presumption (closest connection) § 4(2) – "characteristic performance."

A contract's validity is to be decided by the law of the place where the contract is made unless it is to be performed in another country.

If the contract is to be performed in another place as intended by the parties, the validity, nature, obligation, and interpretation are governed by the location of performance.

Freedom of contract dominates in most states, with some restrictions (2nd Restatement).

Juenger – parties should be free to select their own rules that reflect commercial practice and the best law without regard for the desires of sovereigns.

Applying choice-of-law rules to specific issues

For contracts, the difficulties and complexities involved have prevented the courts from formulating precise rules, which provide satisfactory accommodation of the underlying factors in situations that may arise.

Courts state the general principle, such as applying the local law "of the state of the most significant relationship," to provide perspective about the correct approach but this approach does not furnish precise answers.

The courts must look at the underlying factors to arrive at a decision.

A statement of precise rules in choice of law is complicated by the variety of facts and issues.

Many of these issues have not been thoroughly explored by the courts. These rules represent general statements frequently used by the courts in opinions and the rationale of the decisions in more recent opinions.

Notes for active learning

Establishing Agency

Agency relationships are generally formed by the mutual consent of a principal and an agent, although not always. An agency can arise as an express agency, implied agency, apparent agency, and agency by ratification. The most common form of agency is express agency. In an express agency, the agent has the authority to contract or otherwise act on the principal's behalf as expressly stated in the agency agreement. Additionally, the agent may possess certain implied or apparent authority to act on the principal's behalf.

Express agency occurs when a principal and an agent expressly agree to enter into an agency agreement with each other. Express agency contracts can be oral or written unless the Statute of Frauds stipulates that they must be written. A power of attorney is an example of an express agency. An implied agency is an agency that occurs from the parties' conduct rather than from a prior agreement between them. The facts determine the extent of the agent's authority.

Implied authority can be conferred by *industry custom, prior dealing between the parties*, the agent's position, and acts deemed necessary to carry out the agent's duties.

Apparent agency (or *agency by estoppel*) arises when a principal creates the appearance of an agency that does not exist. Where an apparent agency is established, the principal is estopped from denying the agency relationship and is bound to contracts entered into by the apparent agent while acting within the scope of the apparent agency. The principal's actions (not the agent's) create an apparent agency.

An *agency by ratification* occurs when a person misrepresents themselves as another's agent when they are not, and the purported principal ratifies (accepts) the unauthorized act. In such cases, the principal is bound to perform, and the agent is relieved of liability for misrepresentation.

Notes for active learning

Contract Law – Quick Facts

1. A **gratuitous assignee** has rights under a contract that *may* be enforced against the **obligor** *until or unless* the assignment is revoked.

2. Where there is a **delegation of duties**, the delegator *and* the delegate are *liable* for the performance of the agreement.

3. Under UCC, a **crop failure** resulting from an unexpected cause excuses a farmer's obligation to deliver the full amount if they make a fair and reasonable allocation among their buyers, which could be allocated *pro-rata* between buyers.

   The buyer may accept the proposed modification *or* terminate the contract.

4. The general rule is that a **contractor** is responsible for destroying the premises under construction *prior to completion*; once the residence is complete, the **risk of loss** shifts to the owner.

5. **Performance is excused** where it is prevented by the **operation of law**, despite stipulations to the contrary; governmental interference makes the contract's performance illegal. The party may be excused from the performance.

6. A **detriment** exists whenever a promisee gives up the **legal right** to do something, regardless of whether they would have done otherwise.

7. Under UCC, a **written confirmation** is sufficient as an acceptance even though it states additional terms *unless* the acceptance is **expressly made conditional on assent** to the additional terms.

8. An **implied-in-fact** contract is formed by *mutual manifestations of assent* (i.e., conduct) other than oral or written language. Even if there is no mutual assent, the parties are bound if their conduct objectively manifests contractual intent.

9. **Assignment and delegation** are prohibited where they would substantially alter the obligor's risks, such as an **exoneration clause**, which effectively holds the obligor accountable (liable) for the obligee's actions.

10. A **novation** substitutes a new party for an original party to the contract—requires the assent of *all* parties and completely releases the original party.

11. **Despite reliance**, a third-party **donee beneficiary** has *no* cause of action against the promise because the promisor's act is gratuitous. The promisor may *not* be held to it *unless* they have directly created the reliance by personally informing the beneficiary.

12. Where there is an **oral condition precedent**, evidence of the condition falls outside the *parol evidence rule.*

Notes for active learning

Relationship matrix

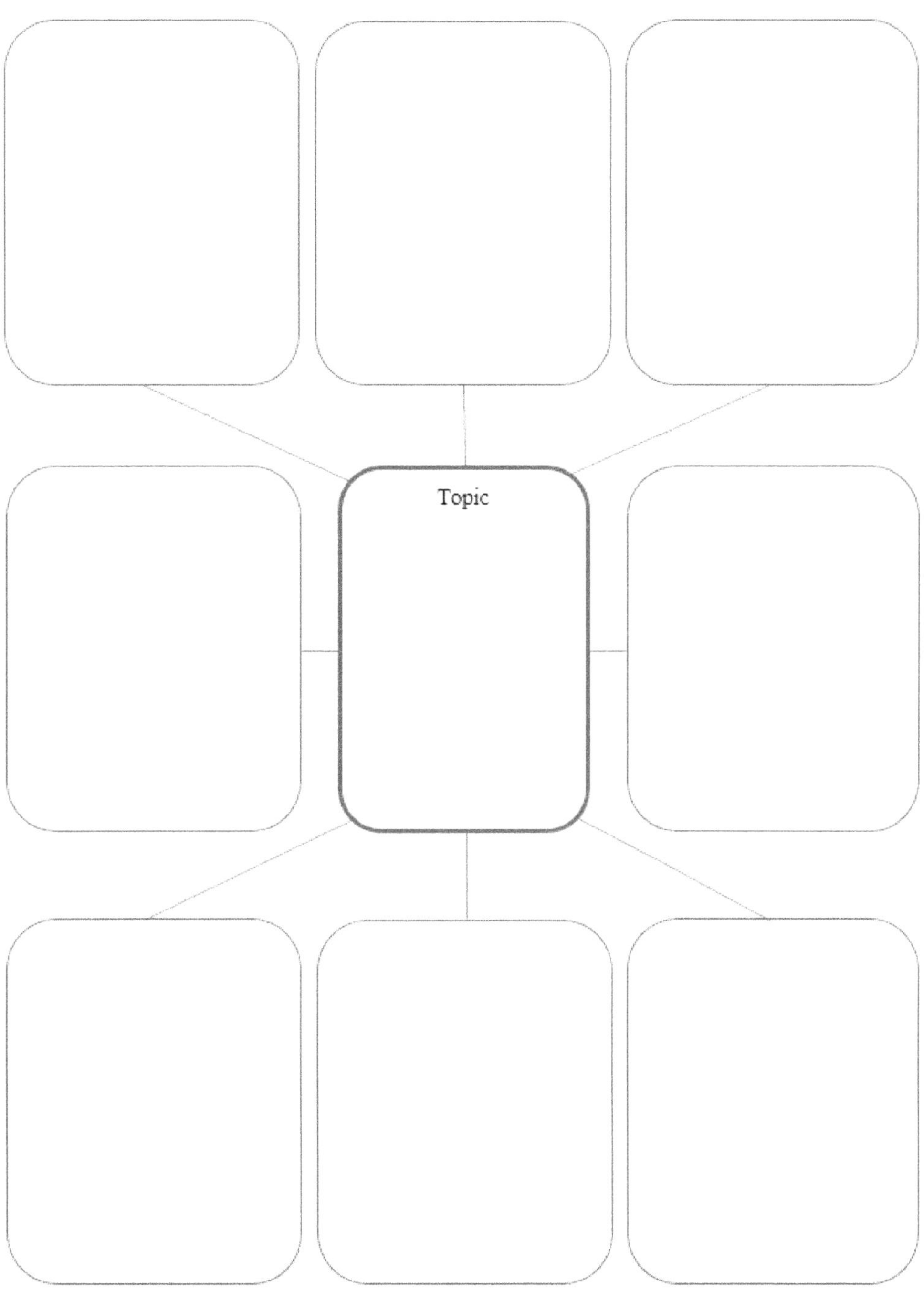

Notes for active learning

Review Questions

Multiple-choice questions

1. Examples of enforceable agreements are:

    I. Sales contracts

    II. Rental agreements

    III. Licensing agreements

   A. I only

   B. I and II only

   C. II and III only

   D. I, II and III

2. Article 2 of the UCC applies to merchants for:

   A. Sales of at least $100

   B. Sales of goods

   C. Sales of services

   D. Commercial leases

3. Contracts made by minors are:

   A. Void

   B. Voidable

   C. Executory

   D. Executed

4. An *agreement* involves:

    I. An offer

    II. An offeree

    III. An offerer

   A. I only

   B. I and II only

   C. I and III only

   D. I, II and III

5. If the potential groom backs out late in an engagement, he may:

    I. Be sued under a breach of contract theory

    II. Counter-sue if he feels he was not to blame

    III. Be responsible for items contracted for the marriage ceremony

   A. I only

   B. I and II only

   C. I and III only

   D. III only

6. In a contract, the offeree:

A. makes an offer

B. tenders an offer

C. promises to do something

D. has the power to create a contract

7. A counteroffer:

I. Terminates the offeror's offer

II. Creates a new offer

III. Binds the recipient

A. I only

B. I and II only

C. II only

D. I, II and III

8. The following is NOT a requirement of an effective offer:

A. The offer must be accepted according to the mirror-image rule

B. The offer must be seriously intended

C. The terms must be definite or reasonably certain

D. The offer must be made to the offeree

9. In the evolution of contracts, the following is NOT true:

A. The use of contracts goes back to ancient times

B. The common law of contracts developed in France around the 18th century

C. The United States adopted a *laissez-faire* approach to contracts

D. None of the above

10. Contracts to engage in illegal activity are.

A. Void

B. Voidable

C. Executory

D. Executed

11. Under common law, an offeror may *revoke an offer*:

A. At any time

B. After the offeree has rejected the offer

C. After the offeree accepts the offer

D. Before the acceptance of the offer

12. The following are requirements for an enforceable contract, EXCEPT:

A. Consideration

B. Contractual capacity

C. Agreement

D. Counteroffer

13. *Consideration* may involve:

    I. Money

    II. Performance of an act

    III. Property

A. I only

B. II only

C. I and III only

D. I, II and III

14. According to the statute of frauds, contracts that are not in writing, but should be, are:

A. Void

B. Enforceable

C. Unenforceable

D. Illegal

15. The following is an example of an equitable remedy:

A. Liquidated damages

B. Punitive damages

C. Tender of performance

D. Specific performance

16. A nondisclosure agreement does NOT:

A. Provide for the equitable sharing of information

B. Swear the signatory to secrecy

C. Usually involve takeovers and corporate deals

D. Protect people that have great ideas

17. A contract to perform an illegal act is:

    I. An enforceable private agreement

    II. Void

    III. Unenforceable

A. I only

B. II only

C. III only

D. II and III only

18. The following have the burden of proof of the incapacity to contract:

    I. The minor

    II. The guardian

    III. The conservator

A. I only

B. I and II only

C. III only

D. I, II and III

True/false questions

19. An offeror must objectively intend to be bound by the offer.

    True   False

20. Contracts are involuntary agreements entered into by parties.

    True   False

21. A contract may be made by implication of the parties' conduct.

    True   False

22. An offer does not need to be communicated to the offeree.

    True   False

23. A contract is an agreement that is enforceable in a court of law.

    True   False

24. In an option contract, the offeror cannot sell to another during the option period.

    True   False

25. The object of the contract may be for any purpose.

    True   False

26. "Are you interested in selling your boat for $8,200?" is an offer.

    True   False

27. Special rules have been developed for electronic commerce.

    True   False

28. A counteroffer is a rejection.

    True   False

29. An offeror may revoke an offer before acceptance after it has been made to the offeree.

    True   False

30. The party making the offer is the offeree.

    True   False

31. The terms of a contract become private law between the parties.

    True   False

32. Contracts entered into by minors are void.

    True   False

33. To have an enforceable contract, there must be an agreement between the parties.

    True   False

34. The UCC, Article 2 governs the sale of goods by nonmerchants.

    True   False

35. If a bride-to-be breaks the engagement, they must return the engagement ring.

    True   False

36. Intended third-party beneficiaries have contract rights.

    True   False

Answer keys

1: D	11: D
2: B	12: D
3: B	13: D
4: D	14: C
5: D	15: D
6: D	16: A
7: B	17: D
8: A	18: D
9: B	
10: A	

19: True	31: True
20: False	32: False
21: True	33: True
22: False	34: False
23: True	35: True
24: True	36: True
25: False	
26: False	
27: True	
28: True	
29: True	
30: False	

Anatomy of a Lawsuit

The Trial Process Overview

A lawsuit is a complicated legal process, whether suing, being sued, or acting as a witness. The legal process can have numerous unpleasant surprises and frustrating delays.

There are at least two parties to every action, and the court dictates the schedule and events. Some things happen in the same order in most litigation; the following chronology shows how a lawsuit proceeds. The actions may be different because of variations between state laws and rules of civil procedure.

At the start of a lawsuit, the legal papers filed in court are the pleadings (i.e., formal declarations of facts, claims, and the relief sought). Several documents become a part of a lawsuit, with some states have different names for the documents.

There are four main stages to a trial:

Pleading stage - filing the complaint and the defense's motions.

Pretrial stage - discovery process and finding of facts.

Trial stage - empaneling the jury, testimony on behalf of the plaintiffs, and testimony on behalf of the defendants.

Post-trial stage - concluding arguments, judge's charge to the jury, jury deliberations, announcement of judgment, motions for new trial or appeal.

Civil cases

A civil case begins when the plaintiff (i.e., person or entity) claims that the defendant (e.g., another person or entity) failed to perform a legal duty owed to the plaintiff. The plaintiff and the defendant are referred to as "parties" or "litigants." The plaintiff may ask the court to tell the defendant to fulfill the duty (i.e., performance) or make compensation (i.e., damages) for the harm done. Legal duties include respecting rights established under the Constitution, federal or state law.

For example, a lumberyard enters a contract to sell a specific amount of wood to a carpenter for an agreed-upon price. It fails to deliver the wood, forcing the carpenter to buy it elsewhere at a higher price. The carpenter might sue the lumberyard to pay the extra costs (i.e., damages) incurred because the lumberyard failed to deliver.

If these parties were from different states, that suit could be brought in federal court under diversity jurisdiction if the amount in question exceeded the minimum required by statute ($75,000.01).

Individuals, corporations, and the federal government can bring civil suits in federal court, claiming federal statutes or constitutional rights violations.

For example, the federal government can sue a hospital for overbilling Medicare and Medicaid, violating a federal statute. An individual could sue a local police department for violating their constitutional rights (e.g., the right to assemble peacefully).

Criminal cases

A person accused of a crime is generally charged in a formal accusation called an indictment (for felonies or serious crimes) or information (for misdemeanors). *On behalf of the people*, the government prosecutes the case through the United States Attorney's Office if the person is charged with a federal crime or the state's attorney's office (or district attorney) to prosecute state crimes.

It is not the victim's responsibility (nor right) to bring a criminal case. For example, the government would prosecute the kidnapper in a kidnapping case, and the victim would not be a party to the action. In some criminal cases, there may not be a specific victim. For example, state governments arrest and prosecute people accused of violating laws against driving while intoxicated because society regards that as a severe offense that can harm others.

When a court determines that an individual committed a crime, that person will receive a sentence. The sentence may be an order to pay a monetary penalty (e.g., restitution to the victim), imprisonment, supervision in the community, or some combination.

Intersection of civil and criminal cases

Civil cases involve disputes between (usually) private parties, while criminal cases are considered acts against the local or federal government. However, some acts may result in civil claims and criminal charges. For instance, a person may be sued for the intentional tort of assault or battery and may be arrested and charged with the crime of assault and battery.

There are times when a criminal act may give way to civil liability, such as when someone is charged with homicide and sued for wrongful death (typically follows the completion of the criminal trial). The criminal charges are punishable by fines, prison time, and other penalties, while the civil lawsuit focuses on recovering money to compensate the victim (or the victim's family) for damages.

Pleading Stage

The complaint initiates a lawsuit

A civil action (as opposed to a criminal or family proceeding, for example) begins with a *complaint*, usually accompanied by a *summons*. A complaint is a legal document that lays out the plaintiff's claims (the person bringing the lawsuit) has against the defendant (the person or business being sued).

The complaint (or *petition*) is the first document filed, which outlines the plaintiff's claims against the defendant. The complaint identifies the parties, sets the legal basis for the court's jurisdiction over the controversy, states the plaintiff's legal claims, relates the facts giving rise to the claims, and sets forth the plaintiff's request for relief. The plaintiff sets forth what they want the court to require the defendant to do, such as pay damages.

The complaint provides the defendant with notice of the factual and legal basis of the plaintiff's claims. Generally, the facts outlined in the complaint are based on the plaintiff's knowledge. The plaintiff may use the phrase "upon information and belief" for facts. The plaintiff may have learned about some facts from others and has formed a good-faith belief that the events are as described.

Most states require that the complaint set forth a *short and plain* statement of the plaintiff's claims. Often, the facts in the complaint are sparse and do not describe all events.

Summons

The summons is an order from the court where the lawsuit will be heard (i.e., litigated). The summons notifies the recipient (defendant) that they have been sued, refers to the complaint (or petition), and sets the time limit within which the defendant must file an answer or seek to have the case dismissed.

The summons describes the consequences of failing to respond promptly. For example, the case may be decided without the defendant, and the decision binds them. In jurisdictions where an action is commenced by service, the action can go on for a long time before the court ever becomes involved.

Failing to respond to a lawsuit on time causes the defendant to be *in default*.

Notice and service of process

The summons is delivered or *served* on the defendant along with the complaint. The summons is usually a form document with a preprinted caption that contains the name of the court, the parties, and a docket number (i.e., the court's identification number). The document informs the defendant that they have been sued; it serves as the *notice*.

                79

Receipt is when somebody confirms their identity or mailed to the defendant; the *service of process.*

The summons, properly served, gives the court power (i.e., jurisdiction) over the dispute and the defendant. The court must have jurisdiction over the parties and issue described in the complaint. The decisions affecting the defendant are binding and enforceable for the litigated controversy.

Answer to the complaint

The defendant's response to the complaint is an *answer*, though some states use a different word. The answer addresses each paragraph in the complaint, and each response will ordinarily take one of three forms: "admitted," "denied," "insufficient knowledge to admit or deny." The answer says what portions of the complaint, if any, the defendant admits to, what the defendant contests, what defenses the defendant may have, and whether the defendant has claims against the plaintiff or others.

An answer may set forth various affirmative defenses, which are legal reasons why the defendant should not be held liable for the plaintiff's damages. Some of these defenses may be the basis of a motion to dismiss. The defendant must answer within a specific time (usually within weeks). If the defendant does not answer the complaint, the court may enter a default judgment.

Following the defendant's response to the plaintiffs' claims, the parties can choose to settle or request a judgment based on the evidence presented, or the court can decide to continue toward resolving the conflict at trial. If there is no judgment rendered, the case proceeds to the pretrial stage.

Counterclaim

If a defendant has a claim against the plaintiff, which arose out of the same circumstances as those that led to the complaint, it should be raised in the answer in a section entitled *counterclaims*. The counterclaim is written like the complaint.

If a defendant asserts a counterclaim in the answer, the plaintiff may respond by filing a *reply*. The reply admits, denies, or asserts that the plaintiff lacks information, just as the original answer did. The reply may assert defenses, just as the answer did.

Crossclaims

Crossclaims arise when two or more parties to the lawsuit, who are "aligned" as plaintiffs or defendants, have their dispute arising out of the same transaction or occurrence. A crossclaim is a claim against a party on the same side of an action.

Rule 13(g) of the Federal Rules of Civil Procedure, a crossclaim must be related to the original action in that it arises from the same transaction or occurrence as the original action or a counterclaim or involves property subject matter of the original action.

The person being sued in a crossclaim file an answer like the original complaint. For example, if Driver B and Driver C are sued by Driver A after a multiple-vehicle accident, and Driver C was injured by something Driver B did, Driver C might file a crossclaim against Driver B within the same lawsuit. The defendant will want to consider the various defenses available to them concerning the claim.

Third-party complaint

Sometimes a defendant who has been sued will have a legal reason for passing liability off to another person. This person may be brought into the lawsuit if the defendant files a third-party complaint. An example is a contract where the third party promises to pay another if the defendant is found liable.

The complaint sets forth the facts giving rise to the defendant's claim against the third party and requests relief. The party sued through a third-party complaint files an answer, similar to the one filed after the original complaint.

Notes for active learning

Pretrial Stage

Discovery

A hallmark of the American legal system is the principle that there should be few surprises during a lawsuit. Since the late 1940s, the federal court system has required disclosing relevant facts and documents to the other side before trial, and virtually every state has followed this requirement. That disclosure is accomplished through a methodical process called *discovery*.

Discovery is the first phase in which the witness gets involved. Discovery takes three primary forms: written discovery (e.g., interrogatories) which must be answered under oath, document production, and depositions (i.e., sworn statements taken before a court officer). The parties exchange documents and other information about the litigation issues during discovery. The information is used in preparing the case for trial. Typically, third parties are involved in depositions, although there are provisions for written discovery and document requests to nonparties in many jurisdictions.

After discovery, the court typically reviews the facts of the case and determines if there is sufficient merit to proceed to trial or encourage the parties to settle. If the finding of facts determines the case to be frivolous or non-substantiated, the case is dismissed. If a substantial basis for the case is determined, the court will meet with and notify the parties of the trial schedule in the *pretrial order*.

Interrogatories and requests for admission

Interrogatories are questions requiring the opposing side's version of the facts and claims. They can be preprinted "form" interrogatories or specific questions asked. Questions can range from the broad ("What happened on Tuesday, June 18, 2021?") to the specific ("Is it your position that the defendant was wearing a blue jacket at 2:30 p.m. on May 13, 2021?"). If the questions asked are not fair or are difficult to understand, the party may object.

Requests for admission are not often used but can be a very powerful tool. They ask a party to admit or deny specific facts about the case, and they carry penalties for not answering, answering falsely, or answering late.

Document production

Each party has a right to see most documents arguably relate to a case. Particularly in more complex medical malpractice or product defect cases, the documents involved can be voluminous. Increasingly, courts are allowing access to computer files during document discovery. In cases where enough is at stake to justify it, courts have even allowed litigants to reconstruct deleted files (e.g., e-mail).

Depositions

Depositions are sworn statements when a person answers questions, and a court reporter makes a transcript of what is said. Depositions can range in length from an hour to weeks. Although attorneys have their strategies for depositions, there are three reasons to do them: to lock people into their stories, to see what the other side has, and to do a "practice trial," that is, to see how a witness will appear and conduct themselves before a judge or jury.

Depositions typically take place outside the courtroom, before a court recorder, with opposing counsel asking questions of the witness. The purpose of a deposition is to give facts, not speculate about what might have happened. Sometimes, "I don't know" is the correct answer. Second, it is human nature to want to explain things but resist the impulse. It is the opponent's responsibility to elicit the answers. The deponent should answer the question asked and not offer additional information.

Settlement avoids litigation

Most civil litigation cases never reach a final trial because a negotiated settlement is reached. Settlement ultimately means the plaintiff relinquishes their right to pursue the settled issue. For legal disputes, settlement can occur before or during litigation. Litigation is the dispute resolution process within the public court system after one party files a complaint and the other party answers. Settlement negotiation can be a formal or informal process. Parties can settle (i.e., agree) during informal negotiation or use a formal process called alternate dispute resolution (ADR), such as *mediation* or *arbitration.*

Some states and the federal system require litigants in civil actions to participate in alternative dispute resolution (ADR) in some form. The parties can agree to binding arbitration, and some contracts (insurance contracts and construction contracts, for example) require binding arbitration.

Often, the terms of the settlement are kept confidential. Sometimes, parties reach a settlement on specific issues in the case while a judge or jury needs to decide other issues. The Federal Rules of Evidence (and most state rules of evidence) provide that most settlement communications are inadmissible in court proceedings. Keeping these negotiations protected gives parties an incentive to have honest settlement discussions.

Typically, the court is either not involved or is involved informally. Judicial approval of civil settlements is usually required when one of the parties is a minor, a class action, or other circumstances that do not typically arise in most litigation.

Most criminal cases never go to trial either. Settlement may occur in criminal cases, though not in the same way as in civil cases. Sometimes, negotiations between the prosecution and defense lead to criminal charges being dismissed or a plea deal being reached. In criminal cases, the judge retains control over plea deals and can reject the agreement.

Motions to position the parties

In many cases, one or both parties try to have the dispute dismissed by motion. The parties present to the court those issues that are not in dispute, either because the parties agree or because the application of the law to the facts dictates a result.

The theory is that if a claim or lawsuit cannot possibly prevail, the parties and court should not waste time or money. Unfortunately, motion practice can be lengthy and expensive.

Summary judgment

In a trial, there are two overarching arguments. The attorneys argue about the law: determining which law applies and whether the law should be changed. Ultimately, questions of law are decided by the judge. The second argument is over the facts of each case, in other words, what happened. A jury usually decides the facts after considering testimony and other exhibits.

In many cases, the parties agree on some facts. When one party believes that there are no important facts in dispute, they file a motion for summary judgment. A typical summary judgment motion has three parts.

1) The facts: The plaintiff presents a version of the facts. The plaintiff usually attaches photos, signed statements from witnesses, and other evidence to support their statements.

2) The law: The plaintiff argues about the state of the law. The plaintiff's attorney prepares a memorandum that discusses the statutes and cases that govern the parties and attempt to convince the judge that, under the law, the plaintiff is entitled to win the case.

3) Even if…: In the last part of the summary judgment motion, the plaintiff anticipates what the defendant argues and tries to prove that the plaintiff will still win the case even if the defendant is correct in their arguments. For example, the plaintiff in a case about squatter's rights might claim they were living on a piece of property for 15 years but anticipates that the defendant will argue that the plaintiff has only been living on the property for 10 years. In this case, the plaintiff can argue that even if he had only been living on the property for 10 years, that is still enough time to win on a claim of squatter's rights.

The defendant responds. In their response, the defendant can show that the plaintiff's assertions about the law are incorrect, or evidence supports more than one version of the facts.

The judge's decision. After the papers and supporting evidence have been submitted, the judge reviews the paperwork and decides. The judge will grant the motion or agree with (in this example) the plaintiff if:

1) the plaintiff's arguments about the law were correct, and

2) even assuming the defendant's version of the facts was true, the plaintiff wins.

The judge will deny the motion if there is evidence that presents facts at trial.

Change of venue

Two basic requirements must be met before a court can hear a case.

1) *jurisdiction*, which means that the court can decide the legal issues affecting the parties' rights.

2) *venue*, which decides whether the court is in the best location to hear the case. Although this may sound unimportant, there are strict rules concerning where a case may be heard.

When one party wants to change venue, they must file a motion for change of venue. A motion for a change of venue ensures that a case is heard in the best location.

Most jurisdictions have strict requirements for the motion, which can be found in that jurisdiction's rules of procedure. Usually, a memorandum of law must accompany this motion, laying out the law and the arguments for why the venue should be moved. There are famous (or infamous) cases in a locality, and a party may wish to change venue so that jurors are less likely to have heard of the case and, therefore, be unbiased. Each state and federal jurisdiction has rules concerning venue

There are often rules about when a motion for change of venue may be filed during a case. If the venue is not challenged at the proper time, a challenge may be precluded.

Statutes of limitations

There are definite time limits to file a lawsuit. It depends upon the state (or federal law) and the offense. Some claims expire within a year after the event. Other claims can be filed decades later (e.g., tax fraud).

There are several ways that a statute of limitation may start, but the common three are:

1) The "date of harm." For example, the day you have a traffic accident will typically start the statute of limitations for suits regarding property damage to your car.

2) The date the harm was first discovered. The harm may lie dormant for a while and be discovered later. For example, hidden property damage until an inspection.

3) The date the harm should have been discovered. This is a less common standard, but in some instances, the period starts when the plaintiff should have discovered the harm, not when they did.

An exception is if the plaintiff sues a government agency. Because the government writes the rules, they have made it particularly difficult to sue them. In some instances, as little as 60 days to file a lawsuit is required to file an administrative complaint before filing a lawsuit.

There is much variation depending on the claim. Some statutes of limitations are:

- Libel or slander – 1 year
- Personal injury – 2 years
- Domestic violence – 3 years
- Medical malpractice – 3 years
- Breach of written contract – 4 years
- Breach of oral contract – 2 years

Notes for active learning

Trial Stage

The trial

If the parties do not reach an agreement or the dispute is not disposed of by motion, the case goes to trial. A trial is the plaintiff's opportunity to argue their case for obtaining a judgment against the defendant. A trial represents the defendant's chance to refute the plaintiff's case and offer evidence related to the dispute. In a civil trial, a judge or jury examines the evidence to decide whether, by a "preponderance of the evidence," the defendant should be held legally responsible for the damages alleged by the plaintiff.

Although a trial is the most high-profile phase of a civil lawsuit, most civil disputes are resolved before trial (or before a lawsuit is filed) via settlement between the parties. This process can include alternative dispute resolution (ADR) like arbitration or dismissal of the case.

The following six main phases of a civil trial is presented in the context of a typical "plaintiff *v.* defendant civil case.

1) Jury selection

2) Opening statements

3) Witness testimony and cross-examination

4) Closing arguments

5) Jury instructions

6) Jury deliberation and verdict

At trial, the attorneys (or the parties, if they are not represented) present evidence and legal arguments, and the judge (or jury) decides the facts. The trial is the other point at which third parties can become involved. The attorney for the party who wants a person to testify may subpoena them for trial. Witnesses can be called to testify at any time, from shortly after the event to almost a decade after.

After both sides present their arguments, the judge or jury considers whether to find the defendant liable for the plaintiff's claimed damages, and if so, to what extent (i.e., the amount of money damages a defendant must pay, or fashion another remedy).

Depending on the type of case, a civil trial may not necessarily focus only on the plaintiff's allegations and the defendant's liability. For example, in most divorce cases, a trial judge decides after hearing allegations from both sides of the dispute and enters a judgment that may favor one spouse on one issue (e.g., child custody) and the other spouse as to another issue (e.g., alimony). Once the judge or jury has reached a decision, the judge orders judgment. The judge may order that one party pay the attorney's fees, although such awards are unusual.

Either party may appeal a judge's decision to a higher court. However, it is unusual for an appeals court to overturn a judge's decision. Settlements usually cannot be appealed if both parties agree to their terms. The process can take from six months to years. Generally, the less money in dispute and the more issues are resolved before trial, the faster the lawsuit.

Jury selection

In most civil cases, either party can choose to have a jury. Whether to request a jury is extremely important. Except in cases that are tried before a judge (e.g., family court cases), an initial step in a civil trial is selecting a jury.

During jury selection, the judge (and usually the attorneys) questions a pool of potential jurors regarding general matters or about knowledge or preformed opinions about the case – this process is *voire dire*. These questions probe personal ideological predispositions or life experiences that pertain to the case. The judge can excuse potential jurors at this stage based on their responses.

Either the plaintiff or defendant may exclude a certain number of jurors by using peremptory challenges and challenges for cause.

A *peremptory challenge* excludes a juror for any reason.

A *challenge for cause* excludes a juror who cannot be objective in deciding the case.

Opening statements

Once a jury is selected, the first "dialogue" in a personal injury trial comes in the form of two opening statements -- one from the plaintiff's attorney and the other from an attorney representing the defendant.

Statements to the jury made first by the plaintiffs' attorney and then by the defense attorneys setting up the circumstances and rationale of the legal complaint (plaintiffs) and the reasons for dismissing the claim (defense). No witnesses testify at this stage, and no physical evidence is ordinarily utilized.

Because the plaintiff must demonstrate the defendant's legal liability based on the plaintiff's allegations, the plaintiff's opening statement is usually given first. It is often more detailed than that of the defendant. In some cases, the defendant may wait until the plaintiff's main case concludes before making its opening statement.

Regardless of when opening statements are made in a personal injury case, during those statements:

- The plaintiff presents the facts of the case and the defendant's alleged role in causing the plaintiff's damages (or reasons to find for the plaintiff) -- walking the jury through what the plaintiff intends to demonstrate to get a civil judgment against the defendant.

- The defendant's attorney gives the jury the defense's interpretation of the facts and sets the stage for rebutting the plaintiff's key evidence and presenting any "affirmative" defenses to the plaintiff's allegations (or reasons to find for the defendant).

When a civil lawsuit involves multiple parties (i.e., three individual plaintiffs sue one defendant, or one plaintiff sues two separate defendants), attorneys representing each party may give distinct opening arguments.

Evidence and arguments

Plaintiff testimony

At the heart of any civil trial is often called the "case-in-chief," the stage at which each side presents its key evidence and arguments to the jury. In its case-in-chief, the plaintiff methodically sets forth its evidence to convince the jury that the defendant is legally responsible for the plaintiff's damages or that judgment for the plaintiff is warranted under the circumstances.

At this point, the plaintiff may call witnesses and experts to testify to strengthen their case. The plaintiff may introduce physical evidence, such as photographs, documents, and medical reports.

In complicated civil lawsuits (e.g., employment discrimination, defective product claims), plaintiffs use expert testimony and documentary evidence as crucial in proving the defendant's legal liability. Documents must be authentic. There are many evidence rules to ensure that the item in evidence is the actual evidence, or at least an accurate copy. The rules of evidence govern what may and may not be considered when the jury decides the outcome of a case.

Defense testimony

After the plaintiff concludes its case-in-chief and "rests," the defendant can present its evidence in the same proactive manner, seeking to show that it is not liable for the plaintiff's claimed harm. The defense may call its witnesses to the stand and present independent evidence to refute or downplay the key elements of the plaintiff's allegations.

Once the defense has rested, the plaintiff has an opportunity to respond to the defense's arguments through a process known as "rebuttal," a brief period during which the plaintiff may only contradict the defense's evidence (rather than present new arguments). Sometimes, the defense may, in turn, have a chance to respond to the prosecution's rebuttal.

Once the plaintiff and defendant each present their case and challenge the evidence presented by the other, both sides "rest," meaning that no more evidence will be presented to the jury before closing arguments are made.

Witness testimony and cross-examination

Whether called by the plaintiff or defendant, witness testimony usually adheres to the following formula:

- The witness is called to the stand and is "sworn in," taking an oath *to tell the truth*.

- The party who called the witness to the stand questions the witness through "direct" examination, eliciting information through question-and-answer to strengthen the party's position in the dispute.

- After direct examination, the opposing party has an opportunity to question the witness through "cross-examination." Cross-examination tries to discredit the witness's story, credibility, or otherwise discredit the witness and their testimony.

- After cross-examination, the side that originally called the witness has a second opportunity to question him or her through "re-direct examination" and attempt to remedy any damaging effects of cross-examination.

Witnesses may only present facts that they observed. A witness can say, "I saw the blue car drive through a red light before hitting the pedestrian," but a witness cannot say something like, "The driver of the blue car should go to jail because he ran a red light and hurt someone," because it is the witness's opinion that the driver should go to jail. Lawyers are not allowed to ask leading questions, such as "Where did the blue car go through the red light?" because it suggests to the witness that this event occurred.

Every witness must be able to be cross-examined. Cross-examination is the part of the trial when one attorney tries to discover untruths or other issues with a witness's testimony. The right to cross-examine stems from the 6th Amendment right of the accused to confront the accuser. It ensures that all testimony is rigorously examined before going to a jury. "Hearsay testimony" are statements about what another told the witness and are generally not allowed when the original person is not in court. However, there are exceptions to this rule.

At the discretion of the judge, each witness can be redirected after cross-examination by either counsel. If critical information is not divulged during the initial testimony, counsel can request to *recall* a witness to the stand for additional questioning and cross-examination.

Judges rule on objections

When a lawyer says "objection" during court, they tell the judge that they think their opponent violated a rule of procedure. The judge's ruling determines what the jury is allowed to consider when deciding the verdict of a case.

A judge can either "overrule" the objection or "sustain" it. When an objection is overruled, it means that the evidence is properly admitted to the court, and the trial can proceed.

When an objection is sustained, the lawyer must rephrase the question or otherwise address the issue with the evidence to ensure that the jury only hears properly admitted evidence. In theory, the jury should disregard the improper question asked, although this can be difficult to do.

An objection is essential to procedure even if it is overruled. Once a lawyer objects to some evidence, that objection is on the record. If the lawyer disagrees with the judge's ruling, they can appeal that decision. If the lawyer failed to object to evidence, they lose the right to appeal, even if the evidence was admitted improperly.

Closing arguments

Like the opening statement, the closing argument offers the plaintiff and the defendant in a civil dispute a chance to "sum up" the case, recapping the evidence in a light favorable to their respective positions. This is the final chance for the parties to address the jury before deliberations.

In closing arguments, the plaintiff seeks to show why the evidence requires the jury to find the defendant legally responsible for the plaintiff's damages or why the plaintiff's case is stronger than the defendants. The defendant tries to show that the plaintiff has fallen short of establishing the defendant's liability for any civil judgment in the plaintiff's favor.

Closing arguments are typically intended to be dramatic and pointed for effect.

Jury instruction

After both sides have presented their arguments and evidence, the judge (in a bench trial) or jury (jury trial) considers whether to find the defendant liable for the plaintiff's damages, and if so, to what extent (i.e., the amount of money damages a defendant must pay, or some other remedy).

Jury instructions are the process in which the judge gives the jury the set of legal standards needed to decide whether the defendant should be held accountable for the plaintiff's alleged harm.

The judge decides what legal standards apply to the defendant's case based on the issues and evidence presented during the trial. Often, this process has input from the plaintiff and defendant. The judge instructs the jury on relevant legal principles, including findings the jury must make to arrive at certain conclusions. The judge describes critical legal concepts (e.g., "preponderance of the evidence"), defines claims the jury may consider (i.e., *fraud, breach of contract, emotional distress*); and discusses types of damages (i.e., compensatory, and punitive) based on the evidence presented at trial.

After the judge provides the jury with specific oral instructions regarding its evaluation of the case, the jury is dismissed to deliberate, in private, the outcome of the case.

Jury deliberation, verdict and judgment

After receiving instruction from the judge, the jurors as a group consider the case through a process of "deliberation" and attempt to agree on whether the defendant should be held liable based on the plaintiff's claims. If so, the appropriate compensation for any damages. Deliberation is the first opportunity for the jury to discuss the case. Deliberations are a methodical process lasting from a few hours to several weeks.

Once the jury reaches a decision (may take hours to days), the jury foreperson informs the judge, and the judge announces the verdict in open court.

Most states require that a 12-person jury in a personal injury case be unanimous in finding for the plaintiff or the defendant, though some states allow for verdicts based on a majority as low as 9 to 3.

If the jury fails to reach a unanimous (or sufficient majority) verdict and is at a standstill (i.e., a *hung* jury), the judge may declare a *mistrial*; the case may be dismissed, or a trial starts again with jury selection.

Following the rendering of the verdict, the court can rule and concur requesting final judgment or determine if a new trial is required or if the case should be dismissed.

Appealing a court decision

Most civil and criminal decisions of a state or federal trial court (and administrative decisions by agencies) are subject to review by an appeals court. Whether the appeal concerns a judge's order or a jury's verdict, an appeals court reviews what happened in prior proceedings for any errors of law or procedure. The losing party cannot appeal a case just because they are unhappy with the outcome; they may only challenge decisions that may have resulted from errors, such as a misinterpretation of legal precedent or reliance on evidence that should have been excluded and not presented to the jury.

If the court finds an error contributing to the trial court's decision, the appeals court will reverse that decision. The parties submit briefs to the court and may be granted an oral argument before the panel of judges. Once an appeals court has made its decision, the opportunity for further appeals is limited. As the number of parties filing appeals has risen substantially, the state and federal court systems have implemented changes to manage the appeals process.

Trials *vs.* appeals

A trial and an appeal have a few similarities but many significant differences. The parties present their cases at trial, call witnesses for testimony, and present evidence (e.g., documents, photographs, reports, surveys, diaries). The jury evaluates the veracity of the evidence and determines the facts of the case; what they believe happened. A jury is sometimes referred to as the "finder of fact."

The judge controls the activities in the courtroom and makes the legal decisions, such as ruling on motions and objections raised by the attorneys. The judge is often called the "finder of law." If the parties have chosen a bench trial rather than a jury trial, the judge makes both fact and law findings.

Appeals overview

An appeal is a review of the trial court's application of the law. There is no jury in an appeal, nor do the lawyers present witnesses or other evidence. The court accepts the facts as revealed in the trial court unless a factual finding is clearly against the weight of the evidence.

Another difference between a trial and an appeal is the number of judges involved. A single judge presides over a trial while several judges hear an appeal, depending on the jurisdiction. At the initial appeals court level, courts may have three to a few dozen (en banc) judges.

However, the total number of judges seldom hear claims together. Instead, appeals are typically heard by panels, often comprised of three judges. In rare instances, the full court may decide to grant a motion for rehearing *en banc* when all the judges on the appeals court hear the case and issue a decision. At the state and federal level, Supreme Courts have from five to nine justices (i.e., justices are judges on the highest appeals court in the jurisdiction).

Appellate briefs

The main form of persuasion on appeal is the written appellate brief, filed by counsel for each party. With this brief, the party that lost in the trial court argues that the trial judge incorrectly applied the law. The party that won below will argue that the trial court's decision was correct. Both parties support their positions concerning applicable case law and statutes.

An appeal is a more scholarly proceeding than a trial. Whereas the litigator must be an active strategist in the courtroom, calling witnesses, cross-examining, and making motions or objections, the appellate lawyer builds their case in the brief before the appeal is heard. Appeals often include a short period for oral argument, but the judges often consume this period with questions for the attorney, prompted by the briefs.

The "record" on appeal

Appeals court decisions turn on the record, which documents what happened in the trial court. The record contains the pleadings (i.e., plaintiff's complaint and defendant's answer), pretrial motions, a transcript of what occurred during the trial, the exhibits put into evidence, post-trial motions, and any discussion with the judge that did not take place "off the record." The success of an appeal, therefore, depends on what occurred at trial. If an attorney fails to get critical, available evidence into the record or object to something prejudicial, the opportunity to do so is lost.

Post appeal

The party that loses in a state or federal appeals court may appeal to the state supreme court or the U.S. Supreme Court. Most states call their highest court *Supreme Court*, though Maryland and New York call theirs the *Court of Appeals*.

Review in appeals courts, however, is discretionary. Because the U.S. Supreme Court receives many more requests for review than practical, they typically grant review only to cases involving unsettled questions of law (e.g., different decisions within the federal circuit courts). The U.S. Supreme Court can only review cases that raise federal or constitutional issues. Cases concerning state law exclusively are beyond Supreme Court jurisdiction. At the highest appellate court, the parties have litigated and had the case reviewed at least once, reducing decisions that are biased or contrary to law.

Notes for active learning

Civil Litigation Timeline

Able v. Baker

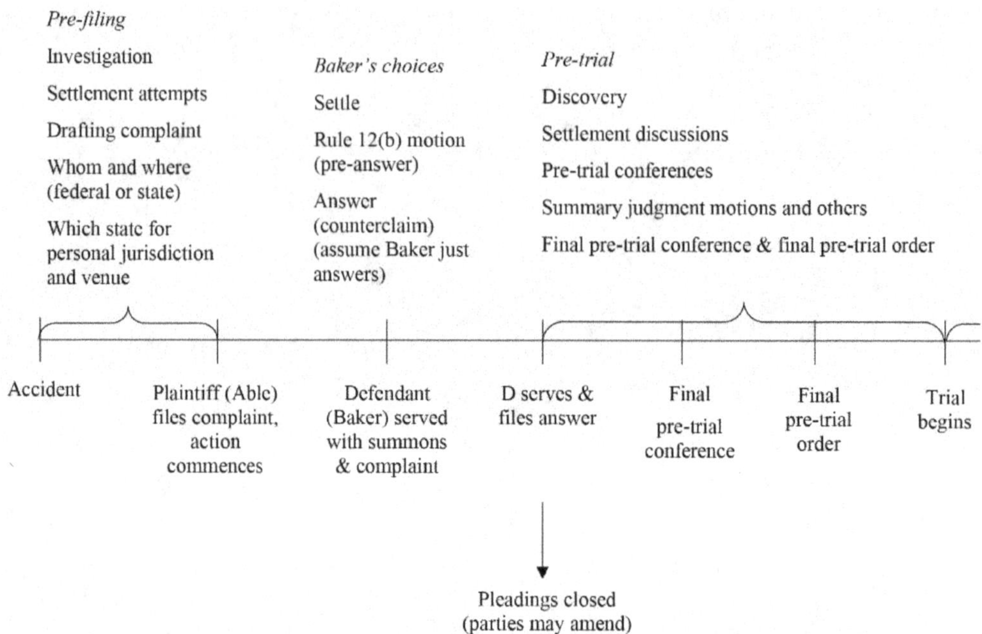

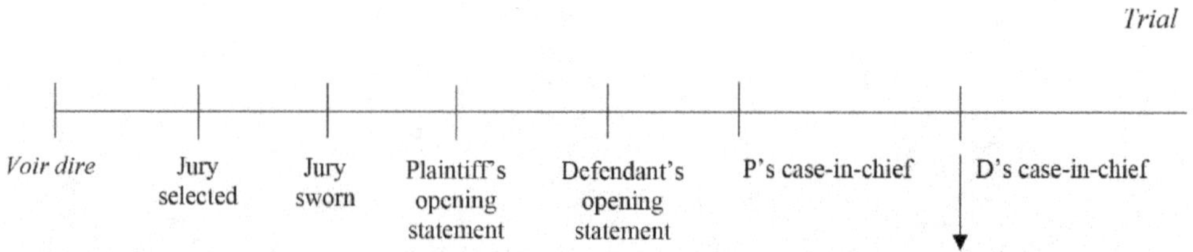

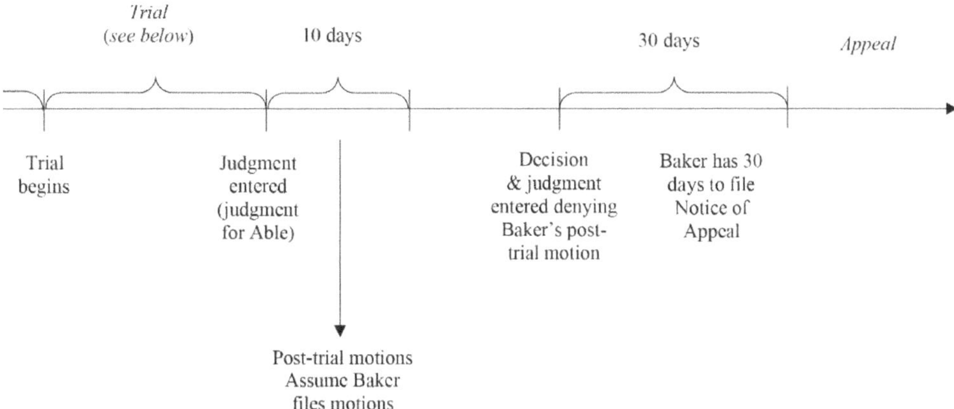

Trial
(see below)
10 days
30 days
Appeal
Trial begins
Judgment entered (judgment for Able)
Decision & judgment entered denying Baker's post-trial motion
Baker has 30 days to file Notice of Appeal
Post-trial motions
Assume Baker files motions

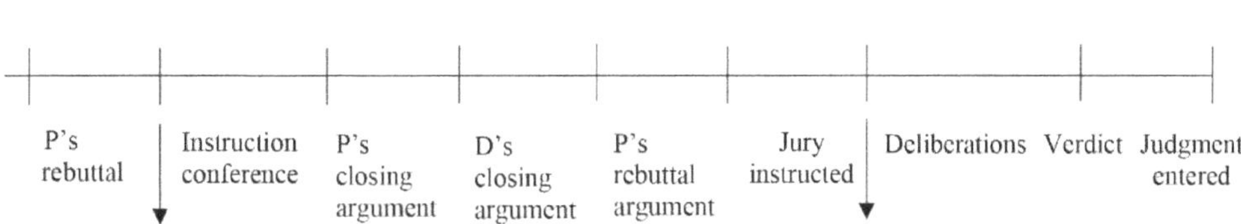

P's rebuttal
Instruction conference
P's closing argument
D's closing argument
P's rebuttal argument
Jury instructed
Deliberations
Verdict
Judgment entered

Notes for active learning

Subpoenas

A *subpoena* [Latin, *under penalty*] is a court-ordered command to produce documents or appear for a proceeding.

The subpoena requires a person to *do* something (e.g., testify, present information) as facts in a pending case.

A *subpoena ad testificandum* requires a person to testify before a court or other legal authority.

A *subpoena duces tecum* requires a person to produce documents, materials, or tangible evidence.

A subpoena may be requested in any matter, but common issues involve divorce, child custody, and personal injury.

Purpose of a subpoena

Under state and federal civil procedure, subpoenas offer parties a chance to obtain information to prove their case.

Criminal attorneys use subpoenas to obtain *witness* or *lay opinion* (i.e., personal experience) testimony from a third party to support the defendant's innocence.

Civil attorneys subpoena individuals and businesses for information that may help settle a claim.

For example, an attorney representing a spouse in a child custody hearing might issue a subpoena to the other spouse to appear in court to determine joint custody arrangements.

Examples of subpoenas include requests for computer files and downloaded material, income tax returns, photographs, graphs, & charts, blood test results, DNA samples, medical, insurance, and employee records.

Authority to issue subpoenas

A subpoena is typically requested by an attorney and issued by a court clerk, magistrate, or judge.

For specific purposes, a subpoena may be issued and signed by an attorney on behalf of the court in which the attorney is authorized to practice law.

If the subpoena is for a high-level government official (e.g., governor, agency head), it must be signed by an administrative law judge.

In some cases, a non-lawyer may issue a subpoena if acting on their behalf (*pro se* litigant).

Serving a subpoena

Depending on the jurisdiction, a subpoena may be served as follows:

Hand-delivered (known as "personal delivery" method);

E-mailed to the last known e-mail address of the individual (receipt acknowledgment requested);

Certified mail to the last known address (return receipt requested); or

Hearing it read aloud.

Responding to a subpoena

A subpoena is part of a court's legal process, and failure to respond is considered *contempt of court*.

The subpoena specifies what is requested or who is to appear.

Subpoena requests for documents are detailed, allowing adequate preparation for testimony at trial or proceeding.

Penalties for failure to comply

A subpoena is a court-ordered command. A person who receives a subpoena but does not comply with its terms may be subject to civil or criminal contempt of court charges and penalties (e.g., fines, jail time, or both).

Civil contempt occurs when a person fails to produce documents requested or fails to obey the terms of a subpoena and, thereby, hinders the judicial process.

Penalties for contempt of court include fines, imprisonment, or both.

Contempt charges apply until the party agrees to produce the requested information and perform legal obligations.

Criminal contempt, usually intended as punishment, refers to disruptive conduct or disrespectful behavior at court.

Criminal contempt includes the refusal to submit documents or other data.

Refusing to produce documents

Defenses for failure to produce documents or appear in court may include claims that the information sought is privileged, lost, violates a person's Fifth Amendment right against self-incrimination, or the requests are overbroad or unduly burdensome.

Alternative Dispute Resolution (ADR)

Alternative dispute resolution (ADR) advantages and disadvantages

Using the court system to resolve disputes can take years and cost thousands, if not millions, for legal fees and expenses. Parties increasingly use alternative dispute resolution (ADR) methods to resolve disputes. The advantages of ADR, as compared to traditional litigation, are the efficiency of costs and time. ADR saves much money, in large part because it saves much time. In commercial litigation, the ordinary business operations of the parties are often disrupted. Moreover, because ADR is faster and less expensive than traditional litigation, it is much less stressful for the participants, which is another advantage.

There are some disadvantages of ADR, however. The process has been criticized as a waste of time by some legal commentators who believe that the same time could be spent pursuing civil court claims. ADR prevents the parties from getting their day in court, and for some litigants, this is a reason to use adversarial litigation. Arbitration awards, for instance, are challenging to overturn on appeal.

Types of ADR

Several processes qualify as *alternative dispute resolution* (ADR). Parties may agree that a negotiated settlement is preferred to investing time and money in protracted civil litigation.

Common forms of ADR include negotiation, mediation, arbitration, conciliation, minitrials, and fact-finding.

Many ADR techniques have little in common except that negotiation is prominent. Mediation and arbitration and are frequently used alternative dispute resolution techniques.

Negotiation

Negotiation plays a vital role in each method, either primarily or secondarily. For example, it is not uncommon for parties to begin negotiations with early neutral evaluation and then move to nonbinding mediation. If mediation fails, the parties may proceed with binding arbitration. The goal with each type of ADR is for the parties to find the most effective way of resolving their dispute without litigation. Many participants in unsuccessful ADR proceedings believe it is helpful to determine that their disputes are not amenable to a negotiated settlement before commencing a lawsuit.

Conciliation

Conciliation focuses on the early stages of negotiation, such as opening communication channels, bringing the disputants together, and identifying points of mutual agreement. Mediation focuses on the later stages of negotiation, exploring weaknesses in each party's position, investigating areas where the parties disagree but might be inclined to compromise, and suggesting mutually agreeable outcomes.

Mediation

Mediation consists of assisted negotiations where the disputants agree to enlist a neutral intermediary. The mediator facilitates a voluntary, mutually acceptable settlement. Their primary function is to identify issues, explore agreements, discuss the consequences of an impasse, and encourage considering the other party's interests. However, unlike arbitrators, mediators lack the power to impose a decision on the parties.

Mediation is referred to as conciliation or conciliated negotiation. However, the terms are not necessarily interchangeable. Conciliation and mediation typically work well when the disputants are involved in a long-term relationship (e.g., married partners, wholesalers, retailers) and intricate problems not easily solved by all-or-nothing solutions (e.g., antitrust suits with many complex issues).

Although some jurisdictions have enacted statutes governing mediation, most mediation proceedings are voluntary. Accordingly, a mediator's influence is limited by the autonomy of the parties and their willingness to negotiate in good faith. Thus, a mediator can go no further than the parties are willing to go.

Since agreements reached by mediation bear the parties' imprint, many observers feel more likely to adhere to decisions imposed than arbitration or court mandates. Disputants who participate in mediation without legal representation are likely to adhere to settlements when the alternative is civil litigation. Attorneys' fees consume a significant portion of any monetary award granted to the parties.

Arbitration

Arbitration refers the dispute to an impartial intermediary chosen by the parties who agree to abide by the arbitrator's award issued after a hearing where the parties have the opportunity to be heard. Arbitration resembles traditional civil litigation in that a neutral intermediary hears arguments and imposes a final and binding decision.

In arbitration, the parties elect to settle future disputes without judicial intervention. The disputants select the intermediary who serves as an arbitrator. Arbitration resembles litigation as parties use arbitration for facilitated settlement negotiations. Parties using arbitration often fail to commence serious negotiations until the arbitration proceedings begin.

In civil litigation, the judicial system is generally chosen by an aggrieved party after a dispute has materialized. Thus, parties to civil litigation have little to no control over who presided in the judicial proceedings.

Frequently, negotiations continue with the arbitration proceedings, the parties' representatives discuss settlement as hearings are underway. Arbitration expedites negotiations since the parties know that the decision is typically final and rarely appealable once the arbitrator issues a decision.

Private arbitration

Private contractual arbitration agreements are used by parties where disputes arise and prefer alternative dispute resolutions compared to a judicial remedy. The arbitrator need not be a judge or government official. Instead, an effective arbitrator is a person whom the parties feel has knowledge, experience, and objectivity to resolve the dispute. In some states, legislation prescribes the qualifications to be an arbitrator.

An arbitrator's power is derived from the arbitration agreement, limiting issues that the arbitrator has the authority to resolve. In many states, arbitration agreements are supported by statutes providing judicial enforcement of agreements and respecting arbitrator-rendered awards.

Statutes governing private arbitration often set forth criteria that must be followed before an arbitration agreement is binding and enforceable by a court. A court typically deems the arbitrator's decision final, and the losing party may only appeal the decision upon a showing of fraud, misrepresentation, or arbitrariness by the arbitrator.

Private arbitration is the primary method of settling labor disputes between unions and employers. For example, unions and employers include a collective bargaining arbitration agreements clause in contracts. The union and employer agree to arbitrate future employee grievances (e.g., wages, hours, working conditions, job security). Many real estate and insurance contracts specify arbitration as the exclusive resolution method for disputes between the parties entering into these types of relationships.

Judicial arbitration

Judicial arbitration is a non-binding form of arbitration. Judicial arbitration is usually mandated by statute or court rules that govern disputes exceeding the jurisdiction of small claims court but insufficient for trial in civil court. A party dissatisfied with the arbitrator's decision may proceed to trial rather than accept the decision. Most jurisdictions prescribe a specific period within which the parties to a judicial arbitration may reject the arbitrator's decision and litigate. If this period expires before either party rejects the arbitrator's decision, the decision becomes final, binding, and judicially enforceable, like a private arbitrator's decision.

Non-binding judicial arbitration in federal court

Several federal district courts also have mandatory programs for non-binding judicial arbitration funded by Congress. For example, the Local Rules of Court may require non-binding arbitration for disputes not expected to exceed $200,000. Since judicial arbitration is mandatory but non-binding, it facilitates settlement negotiations. Arbitration reduces civil court calendars that may have hundreds of lawsuits to improve judicial efficiency.

The policy is that by mandating nonbinding arbitration, the parties value a negotiated settlement. Seldom do litigants receive everything demanded in their petitions or complaints. Private and judicial arbitration is generally less costly and more time-efficient than formal civil litigation. The typical arbitration takes 4 to 5 months, while litigation may take years. The cost of arbitration is minimal compared to civil trials since the American Arbitration Association charges a nominal filing fee. The arbitrator may work without a fee to broaden their professional experience.

Minitrials

A minitrial is a process by which the attorneys present a brief version of the case to a panel, often comprised of the clients and a neutral intermediary who chairs the process. Expert witnesses (or lay witnesses) present the case. After the presentation, the clients, typically top management representatives, attempt to negotiate a settlement. If a negotiated settlement is not reached, the parties may allow the intermediary to mediate the dispute or render a non-binding advisory opinion regarding the likely outcome if tried in civil court.

Businesses use minitrials to resolve large-scale disputes involving product liability, antitrust issues, billion-dollar construction contracts, and mass tort or disaster litigation. Minitrials are effective because they bring top management together to negotiate the legal issues underlying a dispute. Early in the negotiation process, upper management is sometimes preoccupied with the business side of a dispute. Minitrials shift management's focus to outstanding legal issues. Minitrials allow businesses a forum for face-to-face negotiations. Management also generally prefers the time-saving, abbreviated nature of minitrials over time-consuming and costly civil litigation. Minitrials expedite negotiations by making them more realistic. Once the parties have seen their case play out in court, they are less likely to posture over less relevant or meaningless issues.

Summary jury trials

Summary jury trials are used primarily in federal courts. They allow parties to *litigate* their cases before an advisory panel of jurors without a final decision as rendered by a jury in civil court. The purpose of the summary jury trial is to facilitate pretrial settlement. A significant impediment to negotiation is a disagreement between the parties (and their attorneys) regarding a civil jury's likely findings on liability or damages. Like minitrials, summary jury trials give the parties a chance to reach a preliminary assessment of the strengths and weaknesses and proceed with negotiations after the advisory jury's findings.

Summary jury trials and minitrials can be scheduled and completed before formal civil cases usually reach the court docket. Summary jury trials are presided over by a judge or magistrate in a federal district court. Evidentiary and procedural rules are few and flexible. For example, a ten-member jury venire is presented to counsel. Counsel is provided with a short juror character profile and given two challenges to select a final six-member jury for the proceeding. Each attorney has one hour to argue their case to the jury.

After counsel's presentations, the presiding official delivers a brief statement of the applicable law to the jury, and the jury retires to deliberate. Juries are encouraged to return a consensus verdict but may return a special report that anonymously lists each juror's view regarding liability and damages. After the verdict or special report has been returned, counsel meets with the adjudicating official to discuss the verdict and establish a timetable for settlement negotiations.

Early neutral evaluation

Early neutral evaluation is an informal process by which a neutral intermediary is appointed to hear facts and arguments by the parties. In some jurisdictions, early neutral evaluation is a court-ordered alternative dispute resolution technique, the option of hiring a neutral intermediary or having the court appoint one.

After the hearing, the intermediary evaluates the parties' strengths and weaknesses and potential exposure to liability for money damages. The parties, counsel, and intermediary then engage in discussions designed to assist the parties in identifying the agreed-upon facts, isolating the issues in dispute, locating areas in which further investigation would be helpful, and devising a plan streamlining the investigative process. Settlement negotiations and mediation may follow, but only if the parties desire.

The objective of an early neutral evaluation is to obtain an initial assessment of the dispute by an objective intermediary with sufficient knowledge and experience to sift through the facts and issues and find the ground shared by the parties and the ground separating them. Much like in the other forms of alternative dispute resolution, the success of early neutral evaluation depends mainly on the party's credence in the process. It also depends in large part on the disputants' willingness to compromise and settle the dispute. Nevertheless, successful early neutral evaluations can lead directly to meaningful negotiations.

Alternative dispute resolution and civil litigation

The procedures and techniques discussed are the most common methods of ADR. However, despite its success over the past three decades, ADR is not the appropriate choice for all legal disputes. Many individuals and entities still resist ADR because it lacks the substantive, procedural, and evidentiary protections of formal civil litigation.

For example, parties to ADR typically waive their rights to object to evidence that might be deemed inadmissible under the court's rules. Hearsay evidence is a typical example of evidence that the parties and intermediaries consider in ADR forums but is generally excluded from civil trials. For example, suppose a disputant believes that they would be sacrificing too many rights and protections by waiving civil litigation formalities. In that case, ADR will not be the appropriate method of dispute resolution.

Exhibit 1: Complaint

UNITED STATES DISTRICT COURT FOR THE
EASTERN DISTRICT OF VIRGINIA

Civil Action No. 20-CV-1234

John Able,	)	
Plaintiff	)	COMPLAINT
v.	)	
Joseph Baker,	)	
Defendant	)	

1. Jurisdiction is founded on 28 U.S.C. § 1332. Plaintiff is a citizen of the state of Virginia. Defendant is a citizen of the state of Maryland. The amount in controversy exceeds $75,000, exclusive of interest and costs.

2. On January 12, 1999, the plaintiff was driving east on Virginia Beach Boulevard in Virginia Beach, Virginia. Plaintiff entered the intersection of Virginia Beach Boulevard and Witchduck Road when the traffic light directing eastbound Virginia Beach Boulevard traffic through the intersection was green.

3. While the plaintiff's car was in the intersection, the defendant, driving north on Witchduck Road, negligently drove his car into the intersection and the plaintiff's automobile.

4. As a result of the defendant's negligence, the plaintiff suffered physical injuries, including broken bones, muscle, ligament, tendon damage, bruises, and cuts. Plaintiff also suffered pain and emotional distress. Plaintiff required treatment at a hospital and was forced to be absent for two weeks from his job. Plaintiff also incurred expenses for physical therapy and continuing medical treatment.

Wherefore, the plaintiff demands judgment against the defendant for $650,000 plus costs and any other relief the court deems just in the circumstances.

Dated: July 25, 2020

                                Gordon Smith
                                Jones, Smith & Black
                                123 Granby Street
                                Norfolk, VA
                                (100) 100-1111
                                Attorneys for Plaintiff

Exhibit 2: Summons

UNITED STATES DISTRICT COURT FOR THE

EASTERN DISTRICT OF VIRGINIA

Civil Action No. 20-CV-1234

John Able,	)	
Plaintiff	)	SUMMONS
v.	)	
Joseph Baker,	)	
Defendant	)	

To the above named Defendant:

You are hereby summoned and required to serve upon Gordon Howe, 123 Granby Street, Norfolk, Virginia, plaintiff's attorney, an answer to the complaint served upon you with this summons, within 20 days after service of this summons upon you, exclusive of the day of service. If you fail to answer by that time, judgment by default will be taken against you for the relief demanded in the complaint.

[s]_______________________________

Clerk of Court

[Seal of the U.S. District Court for the

Eastern District of Virginia]

Dated: July 25, 2020

Exhibit 3: Answer

UNITED STATES DISTRICT COURT FOR THE

EASTERN DISTRICT OF VIRGINIA

Civil Action No. 20-CV-1234

John Able,	)	
Plaintiff	)	ANSWER
v.	)	
Joseph Baker,	)	
Defendant	)	

1. Defendant admits the allegations in paragraph 1 of the plaintiff's complaint.

2. Defendant admits that plaintiff was driving east on Virginia Beach Boulevard. Defendant has insufficient information to admit or deny the other allegations in paragraph 2.

3. Defendant denies the allegations in paragraph 3.

4. Defendant denies that plaintiff suffered injury as a result of any negligence by the defendant. Defendant has insufficient information to admit or deny the remaining allegations in paragraph 4.

Wherefore, defendant asks that plaintiff take nothing by this action, plus any other relief the court deems.

Dated: September 3, 2020

____

Austin Powers

Powers & Evil

321 Granby Street

Norfolk, VA

(100) 000-0000

Attorneys for Defendant

Exhibit 4: Judgment in a civil case

UNITED STATES DISTRICT COURT FOR THE

EASTERN DISTRICT OF VIRGINIA

Civil Action No. 20-CV-1234

John Able,	)	
Plaintiff	)	JUDGMENT IN A CIVIL CASE
v.	)	
Joseph Baker,	)	
Defendant	)	

Judgment is to be entered as follows:

Upon the jury's verdict, plaintiff John Able is awarded $200,000 damages from defendant, Joseph Baker, plus costs.

Dated: February 8, 2021

[s]______________________________

Clerk of Court

Exhibit 5: Notice of appeal

UNITED STATES DISTRICT COURT FOR THE

EASTERN DISTRICT OF VIRGINIA

Civil Action No. 20-CV-1234

John Able,	)	
Plaintiff	)	NOTICE OF APPEAL
v.	)	
Joseph Baker,	)	
Defendant	)	

Defendant gives notice that he is appealing the court's judgment entered February 8, 2000.

Dated: February 28, 2021

                                      ____

Austin Powers

Powers & Evil

321 Granby Street

Norfolk, VA

(100) 000-0000

Attorneys for Defendant

Exhibit 6: Docket

UNITED STATES DISTRICT COURT FOR THE
EASTERN DISTRICT OF VIRGINIA

Civil Action No. 20-CV-1234

John Able,	)
Plaintiff	)
v.	)
Joseph Baker,	)
Defendant	)

DOCKET

7/25/20 – Plaintiff files Complaint; Summons issues.

8/23/20 – Return of Summons, Defendant served summons and complaint.

9/3/20 – Defendant files Answer.

[Omissions up to judgment]

2/8/21 – Enter Judgment: Upon the jury's verdict, plaintiff John Able is awarded $300,000 damages from defendant, Joseph Baker, plus costs.

2/28/21 – Defendant files Notice of appeal.

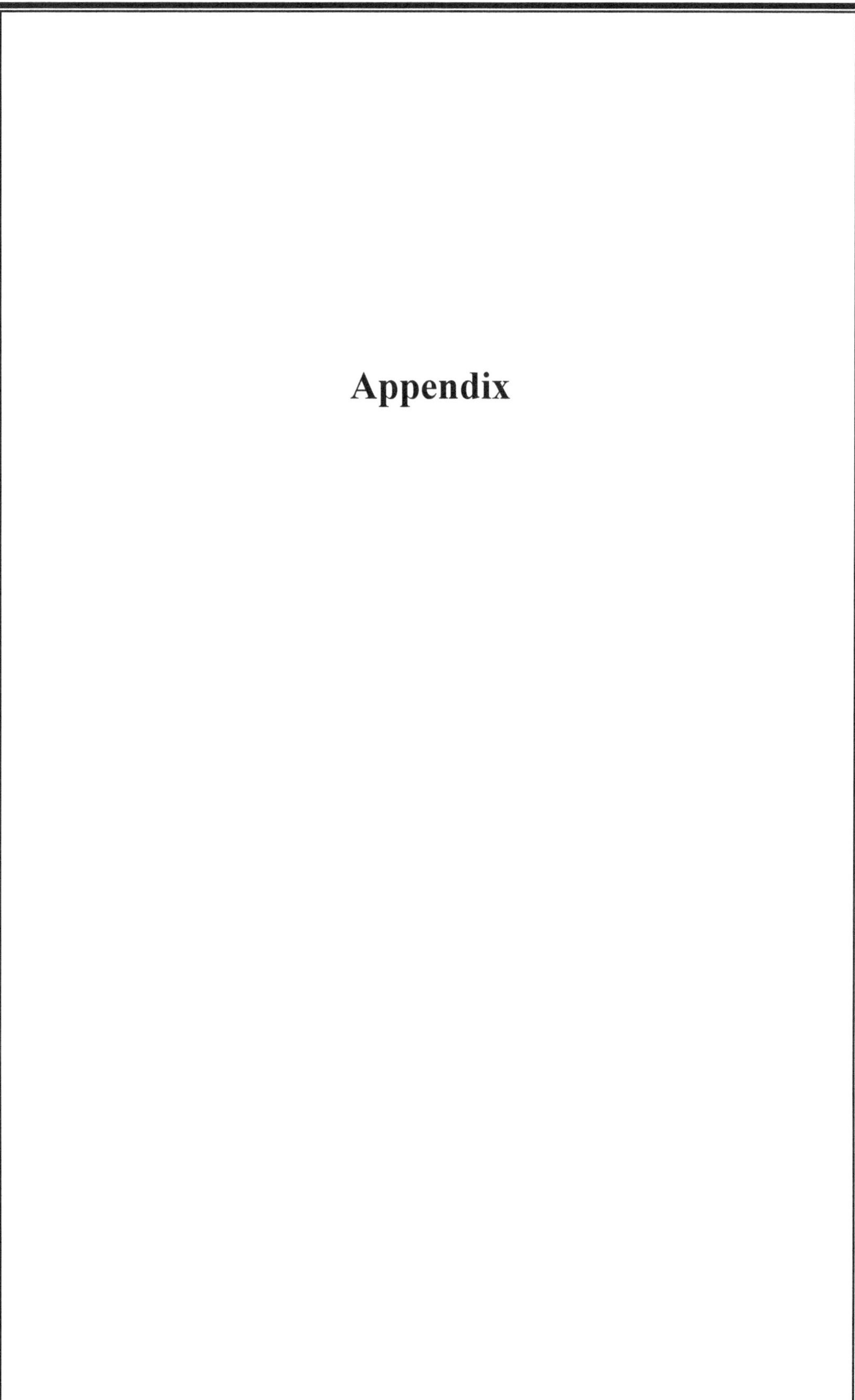

Appendix

Overview of American Law

History of American law

As the American colonies were settled, they relied on the English legal system, known as *common law*.

Principles announced in case decisions are precedent (i.e., guidance) for judges deciding similar disputes.

Three separate courts were established to resolve disputes:

1) Law courts

Before 1066, the local lord was in charge of the locality and resolved disputes as he saw fit.

After the Norman Conquest (1066), these localized courts were replaced with a uniform law system.

Followers of William the Conqueror were appointed to administer justice uniformly in courts of law.

The focus was on procedure rather than the merits of the case.

Damages were in the form of monetary relief or compensation.

2) Chancery (equity) courts

Addressed situations where the result in the law court was unfair or could not be corrected by monetary awards (e.g., injunction).

Equity courts focus on the merits of the case rather than strict adherence to procedure.

Remedies are shaped to fit each dispute.

3) Merchant courts for trade disputes

Rules were developed by the merchants who traveled throughout Europe to resolve disputes that uniformly arose from trade.

Rules evolved to the law of merchants based upon common trade practice and usage.

Eventually, separate merchant courts adjudicated trade disputes.

Adoption of English common law in America

Except for Louisiana, states base their legal systems primarily on English common law.

The law, equity, and merchant courts have been merged.

Most U.S. courts permit the aggrieved party to seek both law (i.e., money damages) and equitable remedies (i.e., injunctions, declaratory judgments).

Civil codes and statutory laws

The civil law system models the Romano-Germanic codified legal system.

Civil code and parliamentary statutes proclaim and interpret the law as the sole sources of the law.

The adjudication of a case is applying the code or statutes to a specific set of facts.

In some civil law countries, court decisions do not have the force of law unless codified into law.

Functions of the law

Although a precise definition of law is complex, it is generally agreed that law must be obeyed and followed, and disobedience is subject to penalty.

The law is often described by the function it serves within a society. The primary functions served by the law in this country are to:

1) keep the peace, which includes making certain activities crimes;

2) shape moral standards, which includes prohibiting certain activities that

   society considers inappropriate or wrong;

3) promote social justice, such as enacting laws that prohibit wrongful
   discrimination;

4) maintain the status quo, which includes passing laws preventing the forceful

   overthrow of the government;

5) facilitate orderly change, such as passing statutes after public debate and input;

6) facilitate planning, commercial laws allowing businesses to plan and

   allocate resources;

7) provide a basis for compromise since 90 percent of lawsuits are settled
   prior to trial; and

8) maximize individual freedom, evidenced by the Bill of Rights.

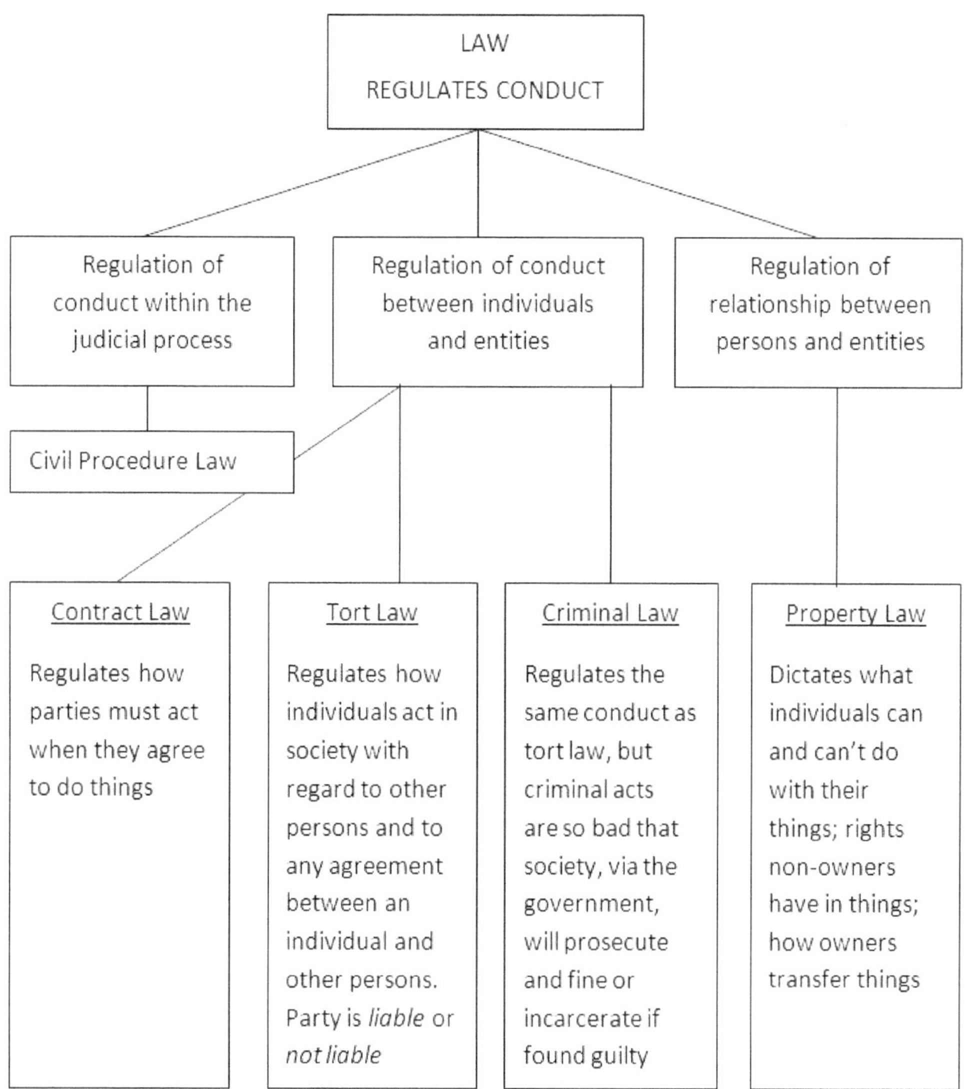
LAW
REGULATES CONDUCT
Regulation of conduct within the judicial process
Regulation of conduct between individuals and entities
Regulation of relationship between persons and entities
Civil Procedure Law
Contract Law
Regulates how parties must act when they agree to do things
Tort Law
Regulates how individuals act in society with regard to other persons and to any agreement between an individual and other persons. Party is liable or not liable
Criminal Law
Regulates the same conduct as tort law, but criminal acts are so bad that society, via the government, will prosecute and fine or incarcerate if found guilty
Property Law
Dictates what individuals can and can't do with their things; rights non-owners have in things; how owners transfer things

Sources of United States law

The foundational source of law in the United States is the U.S. Constitution, which establishes the federal government and enumerates its powers. The U.S. Constitution is *the supreme law of the land*. Therefore, any local, state, or federal law conflicting with the Constitution is void and unenforceable.

Powers not given to the federal government are reserved to the states. State constitutions establish state governments and enumerate their powers.

Treaties are international agreements entered into with other countries, executed by the President with *advice and consent* from the Senate.

Statutes and *ordinances* are codified laws and are created by legislative bodies. Statutes are interpreted and enforced by two types of agency action.

> *Rulemaking* – the adoption of rules and regulations by the agency defining the requirements of a statute. For example, the definition of gross income under the statute is less than one page, but the IRS regulations for this term are dozens of pages.

> *Decisionmaking* – agencies resolve disputes arising under the rules, regulations, and authorizing statute.

Codified laws establish courses of conduct that covered parties must follow. They are written laws (i.e., statutes) enacted by the legislative branch to define acceptable conduct by its citizens. For example, U.S. Congress empowered the commerce clause to regulate commerce between the states and with the Indian nations (e.g., antitrust, bankruptcy). The state legislature has similar power to regulate activity within its borders (e.g., workers compensation, uniform commercial, licenses). State legislatures delegate some power to municipalities, school districts, and others. (e.g., ordinances for building codes, zoning, traffic).

Administrative rules and regulations come from bureaucracies created by the legislative and executive branches of government. Agencies interpret and enforce statutes enacted by legislation (e.g., Congress enacted a statute authorizing the collection of income taxes). For example, the IRS is the administrative agency charged with interpreting and enforcing the income tax statute.

Executive orders are issued by the President and state governors and regulate the conduct of those on whom the executive orders are focused.

Judicial decisions are written opinions of a judge or justice deciding the dispute before setting forth the reasons for the decision. These decisions resolve the dispute and serve as a precedent for the resolution of a future similar dispute. Judicial decisions are often created by appellate courts that resolve legal controversies. An appellate court issues decisions that state the holding of the case and the rationale used by the court in reaching that decision.

Priority of law in the United States

1) U.S. Constitution takes precedence over all other laws (i.e., *the supreme law of the land*).

2) Federal statutes take precedence over federal regulations.

3) Federal law takes precedence over state law, where the state law conflicts.

4) State constitution represents the highest authority in the state, state statutes, then state regulations.

Values-based law

Moral values address fundamental questions of right and wrong. For example, laws against murder protect life. However, not every immoral act breaks the law (e.g., lying to a friend).

Economic values address the accumulation, preservation, use, and distribution of wealth. For example, laws against shoplifting protect property. In addition, the law encourages homeownership by giving tax benefits to incentivize people to borrow and buy a home.

Political values address the relationship between government and individuals (e.g., voting, criminal law).

Social values address issues important to society (e.g., free public education).

Many laws combine values. For example, consider laws against theft. The laws address *moral* (e.g., stealing), *economic* (e.g., protection of property), *political* (punishment for violating criminal statutes), and *social issues* (e.g., respecting the property of others).

The doctrine of *stare decisis*

Court decisions become guidance or precedent for future cases. Lower courts must follow precedent set by higher courts.

The precedent of another jurisdiction does not bind courts in other jurisdictions.

Adherence to *stare decisis* promotes uniformity and predictability of the legal system.

Constitution of the United States of America

U.S. Constitution established a form of the federal government with three branches:

1) Legislative to enact laws – Congress consists of the House of Representatives and Senate.

2) Executive to enforce the laws – President, Vice President, and administrative agencies.

3) Judicial to interpret and determine the validity of laws – courts.

Powers given to the federal government are enumerated or designated powers set forth in the Constitution. All other powers not enumerated in the Constitution are reserved for the states. The emphasis is to protect the rights of individuals (i.e., civil liberties).

Federalism and delegated powers

Federalism – the power to govern is shared by one central or federal government and the 50 states

Delegated (or Enumerated) Powers – those powers set forth in the Constitution assigned to the federal government. Enumerated powers authorize the federal government to regulate specific national and international affairs.

Reserved Powers – those powers not delegated to the federal government are reserved for the states.

The doctrine of separation of powers

Article I establishes a bicameral legislature – establishes Congress.

1) House of Representatives, where each state has representation based on population.

2) Senate, where each state is represented equally with two Senators.

Article II establishes the offices of the President and Vice President and describes requirements and how elected.

Article III establishes a judiciary to hear and resolve legal disputes.

Checks and balances

Checks and balances are included in the federal government system so that no branch becomes too powerful.

1) Judiciary may examine the acts of the Congress and President to determine whether they comply with Constitution provisions.

2) President enters treaties with foreign nations with the advice and consent of the Senate.

Supremacy clause

The Constitution, treaties, federal laws, and regulations are the supreme law of the land.

To the extent state and local laws conflict with federal law, they are preempted.

Some areas of governance are exclusively the federal government's (e.g., postage, coining money, national defense).

Some areas of governance are concurrent where both the state and federal governments share powers (e.g., environmental protection).

Commerce clause

Congress granted the power to regulate trade with foreign governments, between states, and with the Indian nations.

Native Americans

1) At the time of its founding, the colonies (states), in the U.S. Constitution, delegated to the federal government the authority to regulate commerce with the Indian tribes.

2) Applicable to the original thirteen states and the territory to become the United States of America.

Foreign Commerce

1) Federal government has the exclusive power to regulate commerce with foreign nations.

2) Typically through treaties negotiated and signed by the President with the consent of the Senate.

Interstate Commerce

1) Federal government the authority to regulate interstate commerce.

2) Originally interpreted, this clause means commerce that moved in interstate commerce.

3) Modern rule allows the federal government to regulate activities that affect interstate commerce.

4) This test subjects a substantial amount of business activity in the United States to federal regulation.

State Police Power

1) The retained powers of the states to govern within their borders are police power

2) The power to enact legislation for health, safety, welfare, morals, and aesthetics.

3) Includes those powers delegated to local municipalities (e.g., building regulations, zoning codes).

Dormant commerce clause

Prohibits state legislation that discriminates against interstate commerce.

Bill of Rights and other Amendments

The Bill of Rights is the first ten Amendments to the U.S. Constitution ratified in 1791 and guarantying fundamental rights reserved for the people.

Freedom of speech

The First Amendment *freedom of speech* protects the right of individuals to speak freely.

The first Amendment divides speech into three categories.

1) Fully protected speech is political speech (e.g., oral, written, symbolic) that the government may not prohibit or regulate (e.g., flag burning).

2) Limited protected speech: may not be prohibited but may be regulated for time, place, and manner.

    a. Offensive speech may be regulated (i.e., FCC regulation of radio and television programs).

    b. Commercial speech such as advertising cannot be prohibited but may be restricted to placement for safety or aesthetic reasons.

3) Unprotected speech: may be prohibited or banned by the government.

    a. Common examples include yelling "fire!" in a crowded place, fighting words, and defamation.

    b. One complicated issue to define is obscenity; what may be obscene may be acceptable to another.

    c. Obscene speech is a category of speech unprotected by the First Amendment.

    d. Obscenity laws prohibit lewd, filthy, or disgusting words or pictures.

Free speech in cyberspace

The Supreme Court held that the Internet be given the highest level of First Amendment free-speech protections.

As a participatory form of mass speech, the Internet deserves the highest protection from government intrusion.

Because the Internet is a global medium, there is no way to prevent indecent material from abroad.

Freedom of religion

The Establishment clause prohibits the federal government from establishing a state religion and has been interpreted to prohibit promoting one religion over another.

The Free Exercise clause prohibits the federal government from interfering with the rights of the individual to worship as desired unless it involves human or animal sacrifice.

Due process clause

No person shall be deprived of life, liberty, or property without due process of law.

Due process applies to the federal government (via the 5th Amendment) and the state and local governments (via the 14th Amendment).

Substantive due process:

1) Requires that laws enacted by the government be clear on their face and not overly broad.

2) Test whether a "reasonable person" could understand the law to comply with it.

Procedural due process:

The government must give notice and a hearing (i.e., opportunity to be heard) to the individual of legal action taken against them.

Equal protection clause

Prohibits state, local and federal governments from denying persons equal protection of the law.

Laws that classify and treat similarly situated persons differently violate the equal protection clause.

Three levels of tests developed by the Supreme Court to address equal protection and what has come to be known as the anti-discrimination provision of the Constitution

Strict scrutiny – a regulation that classifies individuals based upon a suspect class (race) generally will not be found constitutional (e.g., granting federal benefit to one race violates Equal Protection).

Intermediate scrutiny – regulation related to protected classes (age or sex) will be permissible so long as reasonably related to a legitimate government purpose (e.g., requiring government engineers to be men violates Equal Protection).

Rational basis – regulations of classes other than suspect and protected will be permissible where the is a justifiable reason for the law (e.g., subsidies to a farmer).

Notes for active learning

U.S. Court Systems – Federal and State Courts

There are two kinds of courts in the USA – federal courts and state courts.

Federal courts are established under the U.S. Constitution by Congress to decide disputes involving the Constitution and laws passed by Congress. A state establishes state and local courts (within states, local courts are established by cities, counties, and other municipalities).

Jurisdiction of federal and state courts

The differences between federal courts and state courts are defined by jurisdiction.[1] Jurisdiction refers to the kinds of cases that a particular court is authorized to hear and adjudicate (i.e., the pronouncement of a legally binding judgment upon the parties to the dispute).

Federal court jurisdiction is limited to the types of cases listed in the Constitution and specifically provided by Congress. For the most part, federal courts only hear:

- cases in which the United States is a party[2];

- cases involving violations of the U.S. Constitution or federal laws (under federal-question jurisdiction[3]);

- cases between citizens of different states if the amount in controversy *exceeds* $75,000 (under diversity jurisdiction[4]); and

- bankruptcy, copyright, patent, and maritime law cases.

State courts, in contrast, have broad jurisdiction, so the cases individual citizens are likely to be involved in (e.g., robberies, traffic violations, contracts, and family disputes) are usually heard and decided in state courts. The only cases state courts are not allowed to hear are lawsuits against the United States and those involving certain specific federal laws: criminal, antitrust, bankruptcy, patent, copyright, and some maritime law cases.

In many cases, both federal and state courts have jurisdiction whereby the plaintiff (i.e., the party initiating the suit) can choose whether to file their claim in state or federal court.

Criminal cases involving federal laws can be tried only in federal court, but most criminal cases involve violations of state law and are tried in state court. Robbery is a crime, but what law makes it is a crime? Except for certain exceptions, state laws, not federal laws, make robbery a crime. There are only a few federal laws about robbery, such as the law that makes it a federal crime to rob a bank whose deposits are insured by a federal agency. Examples of other federal crimes are the transport of illegal drugs into the country or across state lines and using the U.S. mail system to defraud consumers.

Crimes committed on federal property (e.g., national parks or military reservations) are prosecuted in federal court.

Federal courts may hear cases concerning state laws if the issue is whether the state law violates the federal Constitution. Suppose a state law forbids slaughtering animals outside of certain limited areas. A neighborhood association brings a case in state court against a defendant who sacrifices chickens in their backyard. When the court issues an order (i.e., an injunction[5]) forbidding the defendant from further sacrifices, the defendant challenges the state law in federal court as an unconstitutional infringement of religious freedom.

Some conduct is illegal under both federal and state laws. For example, federal laws prohibit employment discrimination, and the states have added additional legal restrictions. A person can file their claim in either federal or state court under federal law or federal and state laws. A case that only involves a state law can be brought only in state court.

Appeals for review of actions by federal administrative agencies are federal civil cases.

For example, if the Environmental Protection Agency, over the objection of area residents, issued a permit to a paper mill to discharge water used in its milling process into the Scenic River, the residents may appeal and have the federal court of appeals review the agency's decision.

[1] *jurisdiction* – 1) the legal authority of a court to hear and decide specific types of case; 2) the geographic area over which the court has the authority to decide cases.

[2] *parties* – the plaintiff and the defendant in a lawsuit.

[3] *federal-question jurisdiction* – the federal district courts' authorization to hear and decide cases arising under the Constitution, laws, or treaties of the United States.

[4] *diversity jurisdiction* – the federal district courts' authority to hear and decide civil cases involving plaintiffs and defendants who are citizens of different states (or U.S. citizens and foreign nationals) and meet specific statutory requirements.

[5] *injunction* – a judge's order that a party takes or refrain from taking a particular action. An injunction may be preliminary until the outcome of a case is determined or permanent.

Organization of the federal courts

Congress has divided the country into 94 federal judicial districts, with each having a U.S. district court. The U.S. district courts are the federal trial courts -- where federal cases are tried, witnesses testify, and juries serve.

Each district has a U.S. bankruptcy court, which is part of the district court that administers the U.S. bankruptcy laws.

Congress uses state boundaries to help define the districts. Some districts cover an entire state, like Idaho. Other districts cover just part of a state, like the Northern District of California. Congress placed each of the ninety-four districts in one of twelve regional circuits whereby each circuit has a court of appeals. The losing party can petition the court of appeals to review the case to determine if the district judge applied the law correctly.

There is a U.S. Court of Appeals for the Federal Circuit, whose jurisdiction is defined by subject matter rather than geography. It hears appeals from certain courts and agencies, such as the U.S. Court of International Trade, the U.S. Court of Federal Claims, and the U.S. Patent and Trademark Office, and certain types of cases from the district courts (mainly lawsuits claiming that patents have been infringed).

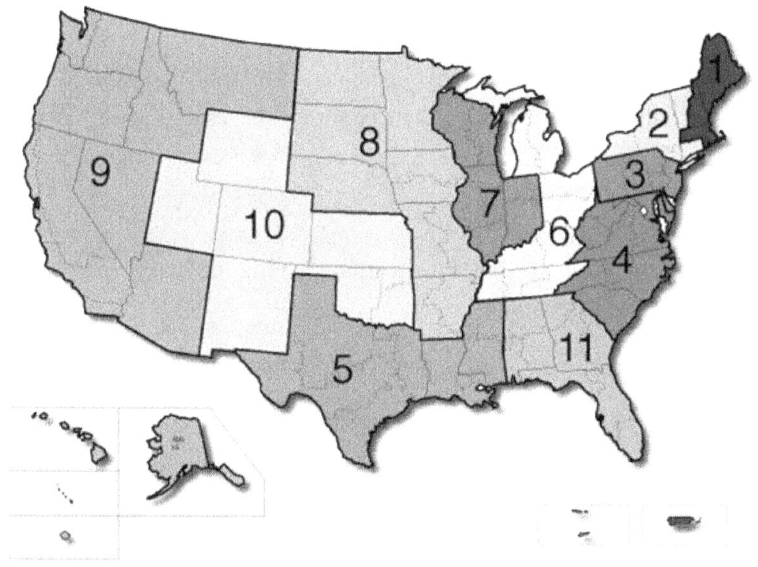

Twelve regional federal circuits

The Supreme Court in Washington, D.C., is the highest court in the nation. The losing party can petition in a case in the court of appeals (or, sometimes, in a state supreme court), can petition the Supreme Court to hear an appeal.

Unlike a court of appeals, the Supreme Court does not have to hear the case. The Supreme Court hears only a small percentage of the cases it is asked to review.

The importance of judicial independence

The founders of the United States recognized that the judicial branch must remain independent to fulfill its mission effectively and impartially. Article III of the Constitution protects certain types of judges by providing that they serve "during good behavior" and prohibits the reduction of their salary.

These constitutional protections allow judges to make unpopular decisions without fear of losing their jobs or having their pay cut.

For example, the Supreme Court's decision in *Brown v. Board of Education* in 1954 declared racial segregation in public schools to be unconstitutional. This decision was unpopular with large segments of society at that time. Some members of Congress even wanted to replace the judges who made the decision, but this Constitutional protection would not allow them to do so.

Article III judges

"Article III judge" denotes federal judges who under Article III of the Constitution are enabled to exercise "the judicial power of the United States" without fear of losing their jobs. They serve for "good Behaviour," which means they can be removed from office only by the rare impeachment and conviction process.

Article III further provides that their compensation cannot be reduced. From a practical standpoint, almost all of these judges hold office for as long as they wish. "Article III judges" are those on the U.S. Supreme Court, the federal courts of appeals and district courts, and the U.S. Court of International Trade.

Constitutional protections for the judiciary

Federal judges appointed under Article III of the Constitution are guaranteed what amounts to life tenure and a fixed salary, not to be afraid to make an unpopular decision.

For example, in *Gregg v. Georgia*, the Supreme Court said it is constitutional for the federal and state governments to impose the death penalty if the statute is carefully drafted to provide adequate safeguards. Even though some people are opposed to the death penalty, Article III protections allowed the Judge to decide without fear of reciprocity.

The constitutional protection that gives federal judges the freedom and independence to make decisions politically and socially unpopular is a fundamental element of our democracy.

According to the Declaration of Independence, one reason the American colonies wanted to separate from England was that King George III "made judges dependent on his/her will alone, for the tenure of their offices, and the amount and payment of their salaries."

Federal judges other than enumerated in Article III

Bankruptcy judges and magistrate judges conduct some of the proceedings held in federal courts. Bankruptcy judges handle almost all bankruptcy matters in bankruptcy courts technically included in the district courts but function as separate entities.

Magistrate judges carry out various responsibilities in the district courts and often help prepare the district judges' cases for trial. They also may preside over criminal misdemeanor trials and may preside over civil trials when both parties agree to have the case heard by a magistrate judge instead of a district judge.

Unlike district judges, bankruptcy and magistrate judges do not exercise "the judicial power of the United States" but perform duties delegated to them by district judges. Bankruptcy and magistrate judges serve for fourteen and eight-year terms, respectively, rather than "during good Behaviour."

Bankruptcy judges and magistrate judges don't have the same protections as judges appointed under Article III of the Constitution. Bankruptcy judges, in contrast, may be removed from office by circuit judicial councils, and magistrate judges may be removed by the district judges of the magistrate judge's district.

Courts and judges

Congress authorizes a set number of judge positions, or judgeships, for each court level. Since the 1869 "Circuit Judges Act," Congress mandated that the Supreme Court would consist of 9 justices. As of 2021, it had mandated 179 court of appeals judgeships and 678 district court judgeships. (In 1950, there were 65 courts of appeals and 212 district judgeships).

As of 2018, Congress mandated 350 bankruptcy judgeships and about 551 full-time and part-time magistrate judgeships. All judgeships are rarely filled at any one time as judges die or retire, causing vacancies until judges are appointed to replace them. In addition to judges in these positions, retired judges continue to perform some judicial work.

Federal judges and judgeships

Supreme Court justices and the court of appeals and district judges are appointed to office by the President, with the approval of the U.S. Senate. Presidents most often appoint judges who are members, or at least supportive, of their political party, but that does not mean that judges are given appointments solely for partisan reasons.

The professional qualifications of prospective federal judges are rigorously evaluated by the Department of Justice (DOJ), which consults with others, such as lawyers who can evaluate the prospect's abilities. The Senate Judiciary Committee undertakes a separate examination of the nominees.

Magistrate judges and bankruptcy judges are not appointed by the President or subject to Congress's approval. The court of appeals in each circuit appoints bankruptcy judges for fourteen-year terms. District courts appoint magistrate judges for eight-year terms.

Qualifications for becoming a federal judge

Although there are almost no formal qualifications for federal judges, there are some informal ones. For example, while magistrate judges and bankruptcy judges are required by statute to be lawyers, there is no requirement that district judges, circuit judges, or Supreme Court justices be lawyers.

However, there is no legal precedent for a president to nominate someone who is not a lawyer. Before their appointment, most judges were private attorneys, but many were judges in state courts or other federal courts. Some were government attorneys, and a few were law professors.

Ethical standards for judges

Judges follow the ethical standards set out in the *Code of Conduct for United States Judges*, which contains guidelines to help them avoid situations that might limit their ability to be fair--or that might make it appear to others that their fairness is in question. It tells them, for example, to be careful not to do anything that might cause people to think they would favor one side in a case over another, such as giving speeches that urge voters to pick one candidate over another for public office or asking people to contribute money to civic organizations.

Additionally, Congress has enacted laws telling judges to withdraw or recuse themselves from any case in which a close relative is a party or in which they have any financial interest, even one share of stock.

Congress requires judges to file an annual financial disclosure form, so that their stock holdings, board memberships, and other financial interests are a matter of public record.

Congress has also enacted a law that allows anyone to file a complaint alleging that a judge (other than a Supreme Court justice) has engaged in conduct "prejudicial to the effective and expeditious administration of the business of the courts" or that a judge has a mental or physical disability that makes him/her unable to discharge the duties of the office adequately.

A complaint is filed with the clerk of the court of appeals of the judge's circuit and considered by the chief judge of the court of appeals. If the chief judge believes the complaint deserves attention, the chief judge appoints a special committee of the circuit judicial council to investigate.

If the committee concludes that the complaint is valid, it may recommend various actions, such as temporarily removing the judge from hearing cases, but it may not recommend that an Article III judge be removed from office. Only Congress may do that, through the impeachment process.

Chief Judges dismiss the great majority of complaints filed under this law because the complaints involve judges' decisions in particular cases. This law may not be used to complain about decisions, even what may appear to be a very wrong decision or very unfair treatment of a party in a case.

Parties in a lawsuit who believe the judge issued an incorrect ruling may appeal the case to a higher court, under the rules of procedure.

Senior judge status

Most federal judges retire from full-time service at around sixty-five or seventy years of age and become senior judges. Senior judges are still federal judges, eligible to earn their full salary and to continue hearing cases if they and their colleagues want them to do so, but they usually maintain a reduced caseload.

Full-time judges are known as active judges.

Docket assignments

Each court, with more than one judge, must determine a procedure for assigning cases to judges.

Most district and bankruptcy courts use random assignment, which helps to ensure a fair distribution of cases and prevents "judge shopping," which refers to parties' attempts to have their cases heard by the judge whom they believe will act most favorably.

Other courts assign cases by rotation, subject matter, or geographic division of the court.

In courts of appeals, cases are usually assigned by random means to temporary three-judge panels.

Notes for active learning

How Civil Cases Move Through the Federal Courts

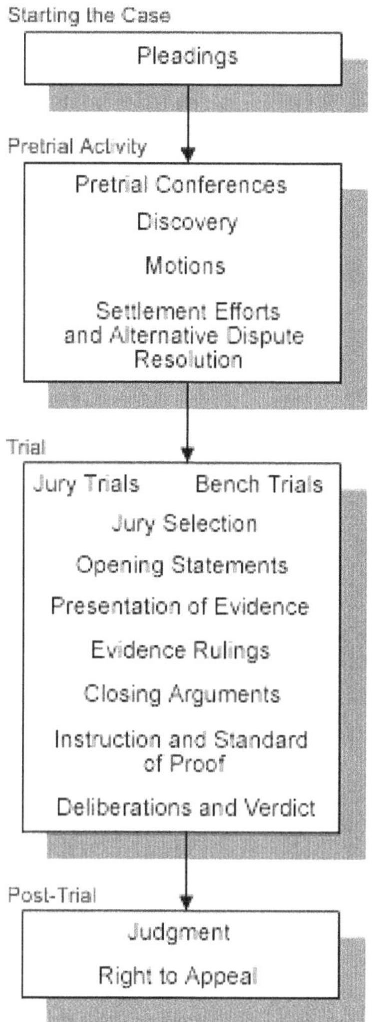

A federal civil case begins when a person, or their legal representative, files a paper with the clerk of the court that asserts another person's wrongful act injured the person. In legal terminology, the plaintiff files a *complaint* against the defendant.

The defendant files an *answer* to the complaint. These written statements of the party's positions are called pleadings. In some circumstances, the defendant may file a *motion* instead of an answer; the motion asks the court to take some action, such as dismiss the case or require the plaintiff to explain more clearly what the lawsuit is about.

Jury trials

In a jury trial, the jury decides what happened, and to apply the legal standards, the judge tells them to apply to reach a verdict. The plaintiff presents evidence supporting its view of the case, and the defendant presents evidence rebutting the plaintiff's evidence or supporting its view of the case. From these presentations, the jury must decide what happened and applied the law to those facts.

The jury never decides what law applies to the case; that is the role of the judge. For example, in a discrimination case where the plaintiff alleged that their workplace was hostile, the judge tells the jury the legal standard for a hostile environment.

The jury would have to decide whether the plaintiff's description of events was true and whether those events met the legal standard. A trial jury, or petit jury, may consist of six to twelve jurors in a civil case.

Bench trials

If the parties agree not to have a *jury trial* and leave the fact-finding to the judge, the trial is a *bench trial*. In bench and jury trials, the judge ensures the correct legal standards are followed.

In contrast to a jury trial, the judge decides the facts and renders the verdict in a *bench trial*.

For example, in a discrimination case in which the plaintiff alleged a hostile environment, the judge would determine the legal standard for a hostile environment and decide whether the plaintiff's description of events was true and whether those events met the legal standard.

Some kinds of cases always have bench trials. For example, there is never a jury trial if the plaintiff is seeking an injunction, an order from the judge that the defendant does, or stop doing something, as opposed to monetary damages.

Some statutes provide that a judge must decide the facts in certain types of cases.

Jury selection

A jury trial begins with the selection of jurors. Citizens are selected for jury service through a process set out in laws passed by Congress and in the federal rules of procedure.

First, citizens are called to court to be available to serve on juries. These citizens are selected at random from sources, in most districts, lists of registered voters, which may be augmented by other sources, such as lists of licensed drivers in the judicial district.

The judge and the lawyers choose who will serve on the jury.

To choose the jurors, the judge and sometimes the lawyers ask prospective jurors questions to determine if they will decide the case fairly, a process known as *voir dire*.

The lawyers may request that the judge excuse jurors they think may not be impartial, such as those who know a party in the case or who have had an experience that might make them favor one side over the other. These requests for rejecting jurors are *challenges for cause*.

The lawyers may request that the judge excuse a certain number of jurors without reason; these requests are *peremptory challenges*.

Instructions and standard of proof

Following the closing arguments, the judge gives instructions to the jury, explaining the relevant law, how the law applies to the case, and what questions the jury must decide.

How sure do jurors have to be before they reach a verdict? One important instruction the judge gives the jury is the standard of proof they must follow in deciding the case.

The courts, through their decisions, and Congress, through statutes, have established standards by which facts must be proven in criminal and civil cases.

In civil cases, to decide for the plaintiff, the jury must determine by a *preponderance of the evidence* that the defendant failed to perform a legal duty and violated the plaintiff's rights. A preponderance of the evidence means that, based on the evidence, the evidence favors the plaintiff more (even if only slightly) than it favors the defendant.

If the evidence in favor of the plaintiff could be placed on one side of a scale and that in favor of the defendant on the other, the plaintiff would win if the evidence in favor of the plaintiff was heavy enough to tip the scale. If the two sides were even, or if the scale tipped for the defendant, the defendant would win.

Judgment

In civil cases, if the jury (or judge) decides in favor of the plaintiff, the result usually is that the defendant must pay the plaintiff money or damages. The judge orders the defendant to pay the decided amount. Sometimes the defendant is ordered to take some specific action that will restore the plaintiff's rights. If the defendant wins the case, there is nothing more the trial court needs to do as the case is disposed of and the defendant is held not liable.

Right to appeal

The losing party in a federal civil case has a right to appeal the verdict to the U.S. court of appeals (i.e., Federal Circuit Courts) and ask the court to review the case to determine whether the trial was conducted properly. The losing party in the state trial court has a right to appeal the verdict to the state court of appeal.

The grounds for appeal usually are that the federal district (or state) judge made an error, either in the procedure (e.g., admitting improper evidence) or interpreting the law. The government may appeal in civil cases, as any other party may. Neither party may appeal if there was no trial -- parties settled their civil case out of court.

Notes for active learning

How Criminal Cases Move Through the Federal Courts

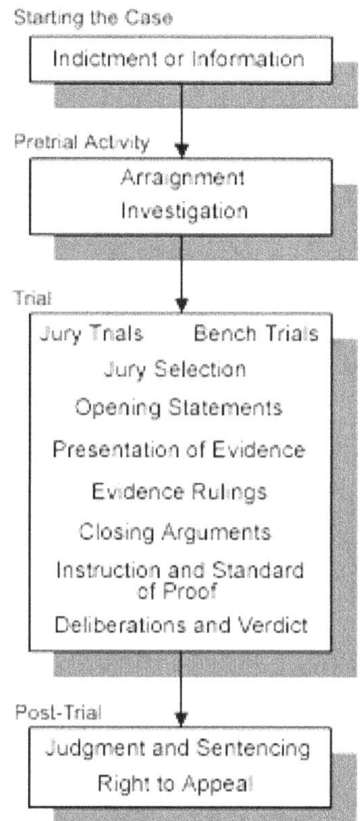

Indictment or information

A criminal case formally begins with an indictment or information, which is a formal accusation that a person committed a crime.

An indictment may be obtained when a lawyer (i.e., prosecutor) for the executive branch of the U.S. government (i.e., U.S. attorney or assistant U.S. attorney) present evidence to a federal grand jury that, according to the government, indicates a person committed a crime.

The U.S. attorney tries to convince the grand jury that there is enough evidence to show that the person probably committed the crime and should be formally accused. If the grand jury agrees, it issues an indictment.

A grand jury is different from a trial jury or petit jury.

A grand jury determines whether the person may be tried for a crime; a petit jury listens to the evidence presented at the trial and determines whether the defendant is guilty.

Petit is French for "small"; petit juries usually consist of twelve jurors in criminal cases.

Grand is French for "large"; grand juries have from sixteen to twenty-three jurors.

Grand jury indictments are most often used for *felonies* (i.e., punishable by imprisonment of more than a year or by death) such as bank robberies or sales of illegal drugs.

Grand jury indictments are not necessary to prosecute *misdemeanors* (i.e., less serious than a felony but more serious than an infraction) and are necessary for felonies.

For lesser crimes, the U.S. attorney issues an *information* that substitutes for an indictment. For example, speeding on a highway in a national park is a misdemeanor.

An information is used when a defendant waives an indictment by a grand jury.

                139

Arraignment

After the grand jury issues the indictment, the accused (i.e., defendant) is summoned to court or arrested (if not already in custody). The next step is an arraignment, a proceeding in which the defendant is brought before a judge, told of the charges they are accused of, and asked to plead guilty or not guilty. If the defendant's plea is guilty, a time is set for the defendant to return to court to be sentenced.

If the defendant pleads "not guilty," the time is set for the trial.

A defendant may enter a plea bargain with the prosecution--usually by agreeing to plead guilty to some but not all charges or lesser charges. The prosecution drops the remaining charges.

About nine out of ten defendants in criminal cases plead guilty.

Investigation

In a criminal case, a defense lawyer conducts a thorough investigation before trial, interviewing witnesses, visiting the crime scene, and examining physical evidence. An important part of this investigation is determining whether the evidence the government plans to use to prove its case was obtained legally.

The Fourth Amendment to the Constitution forbids unreasonable searches and seizures. To enforce this protection, the Supreme Court has decided that illegally seized evidence cannot be used at trial for most purposes.

For example, if the police seize evidence from a defendant's home without a search warrant, the lawyer for the defendant can ask the court to exclude the evidence from use at trial. The court holds a hearing to determine whether the search was unreasonable.

If the court rules that key evidence was seized illegally and cannot be used, the government often drops the charges against the defendant.

If the government has a strong case and the court ruled that the evidence was obtained legally, the defendant may decide to plead guilty rather than go to trial, where a conviction is likely.

Deliberations and verdict

After receiving its instructions from the judge, the jury retires to the jury room to discuss the evidence and reach a verdict (a decision on the factual issues). A criminal jury verdict must be unanimous; all jurors must agree that the defendant is guilty or not guilty.

If the jurors cannot agree, the judge declares a mistrial, and the prosecutor must decide whether to ask the court to dismiss the case or have it presented to another jury.

Judgment and sentencing

In federal criminal cases, if the jury (or judge, if there is no jury) decides that the defendant is guilty, the judge sets a date for a sentencing hearing. In federal criminal cases, the jury does not decide whether the defendant will go to prison or for how long; the judge does.

In federal death penalty cases, the jury does decide whether the defendant will receive a death sentence. Sentencing statutes passed by Congress control the judge's sentencing decision. Additionally, judges use Sentencing Guidelines, issued by the U.S. Sentencing Commission, as a source of advice as to the proper sentence. The guidelines consider the nature of the offense and the offender's criminal history.

A presentence report, prepared by one of the court's probation officers, provides the judge with information about the offender and the offense, including the sentence recommended by the guidelines. After determining the sentence, the judge signs a judgment, including the plea, the verdict, and sentence.

Right to appeal

A defendant who is found guilty in a federal criminal trial has a right to appeal the decision to the U.S. court of appeals, that is, ask the court of appeals to review the case to determine whether the trial was conducted properly. The grounds for appeal are usually that the district judge is said to have made an error, either in a procedure (admitting improper evidence, for example) or interpreting the law.

A defendant who pled guilty may not appeal the conviction.

A defendant who pled guilty may have the right to appeal their sentence.

The government may not appeal if a defendant in a criminal case is found not guilty because the Double Jeopardy Clause of the Fifth Amendment to the Constitution provides that no person shall "be twice put in jeopardy of life or limb" for the same offense.

This reflects society's belief that, even if a subsequent trial might finally find a defendant guilty, it is not proper for the government to harass an acquitted defendant through repeated retrials.

However, the government may sometimes appeal a sentence.

Notes for active learning

How Civil and Criminal Appeals Move Through the Federal Courts

Assignment of Judges

Alternative Dispute Resolution (ADR)

Review of Lower Court Decision

Oral Argument

Decision

The Supreme Court of the United States

Assignment of judges

The courts of appeals usually assign cases to a panel of three judges. The panel decides the case for the entire court. Sometimes, when the parties request it or a question of unusual importance, the judges on the appeals court assemble *en banc* (a rare event).

Review of a lower court decision

In making its decision, the panel reviews key parts of the record. The record consists of the documents filed in the case at trial and the transcript of the trial proceedings. The panel learns about the lawyers' legal arguments from the lawyers' briefs.

Briefs are written documents that each side submits to explain its case and tell why the court should decide in its favor.

Oral argument

If the court permits oral argument, the lawyers for each side have a limited amount of time (typically between 15 to 30 minutes) to argue (i.e., advocate and explain) their case to the judges (or justices at the highest court in the jurisdiction) in a formal courtroom session. The judges (or justices for the highest court in the jurisdiction) frequently question the attorneys about the relevant law as it applies to the facts and issues in the case before them.

A court of appeals differs from the federal trial courts. There are no jurors, witnesses, or court reporters. The lawyers for each side, but not the parties, are usually present in the courtroom.

Decision

After the submission of briefs and oral arguments, the judges discuss the case privately, consider relevant *precedents* (court decisions from higher courts in prior cases with similar facts and legal issues), and reach a decision. Courts are required to follow precedents.

For example, a U.S. court of appeals must follow the U.S. Supreme Court's decisions; a district court must follow the decisions of the U.S. Supreme Court and the decisions of the court of appeals of its circuit.

Courts are influenced by decisions they are not required to follow, such as the decisions of other circuits. Courts follow precedent unless they set forth reasons for the diversion.

At least two of the three judges on the panel must agree on a decision. One judge who agrees with the decision is chosen to write an opinion, which announces and explains the decision.

If a judge on the panel disagrees with the majority's opinion, the judge may write a dissent, giving reasons for disagreeing.

Many appellate opinions are published in books of opinions, called reporters. The opinions are read carefully by other judges and lawyers looking for precedents to guide them in their cases.

The accumulated judicial opinions make up a body of law known as *case law*, which is usually an accurate predictor of how future cases will be decided.

For decisions that the judges believe are important to the parties and contribute little to the law, the appeals courts frequently use short, unsigned opinions that often are not published.

If the court of appeals decides that the trial judge incorrectly interpreted the law or followed incorrect procedures, it reverses the district court's decision.

For example, the court of appeals could hold that the district judge allowed the jury to base its decision on evidence that never should have been admitted, and thus the defendant cannot be guilty.

Most of the time, courts of appeals uphold, rather than the reverse, district court decisions.

Sometimes when a higher court reverses the decision of the district court, it sends the case back (i.e., *remand* the case) to the lower court for another trial.

For example, *Miranda v. Arizona* case (1966), the Supreme Court ruled 5-4 that Ernesto Miranda's confession could not be used as evidence because he had not been advised of his right to remain silent or of his right to have a lawyer present during questioning.

However, the government did have other evidence against him. The case was remanded for a new trial, in which the improperly obtained confession was not used as evidence, but the other evidence convicted Miranda.

The Supreme Court of the United States

The Supreme Court is the highest in the nation. It is a different kind of appeals court; its major function is not correcting errors made by trial judges but clarifying the law in cases of national importance or when lower courts disagree about interpreting the Constitution or federal laws.

The Supreme Court does not have to hear every case that it is asked to review. Each year, losing parties ask the Supreme Court to review about 8,000 cases.

Almost all cases come to the Court as a *petition for writ of certiorari.* The court selects only about 80 to 120 of the most significant cases to review with oral arguments.

Supreme Court decisions establish a precedent for interpreting the Constitution and federal laws; holdings that state and federal courts must follow.

The power of judicial review makes the Supreme Court's role in our government vital. Judicial review is the power of a court when deciding a case to declare that a law passed by a legislature or action by the executive branch is invalid because it is inconsistent with the Constitution.

Although district courts, courts of appeals, and state courts can exercise the power of judicial review, their decisions about federal law are always subject, on appeal, to review by the Supreme Court.

When the Supreme Court declares a law unconstitutional, its decision can only be overruled by a later decision of the Supreme Court or Amendment to the Constitution.

Seven of the twenty-seven Amendments to the Constitution have invalidated the decisions of the Supreme Court. However, most Supreme Court cases do not concern the constitutionality of laws, but the interpretation of laws passed by Congress.

Although Congress has steadily increased the number of district and appeals court judges over the years, the Supreme Court has remained the same size since 1869. It consists of a Chief Justice and eight associate justices.

Like the federal court of appeals and federal district judges, the Supreme Court justices are appointed by the President with the Senate's *advice and consent.*

Unlike the judges in the courts of appeals, Supreme Court justices never sit on panels. Absent recusal, nine justices hear cases, and a majority ruling decides cases.

The Supreme Court begins its annual session, or term, on the first Monday of October. The term lasts until the Court has announced its decisions in cases where it has heard an argument that term—usually late June or early July.

During the term, the Court, sitting for two weeks at a time, hears oral arguments on Monday through Wednesday and holds private conferences to discuss the cases, reach decisions, and begin preparing the written opinions that explain its decisions.

Most decisions and opinions are released in the late spring and early summer.

Notes for active learning

Standards of review for federal courts

Standard of review	*De novo*	Clearly erroneous	Abuse of discretion
Type of decision under review	Question of the law	Question of fact	Discretionary action
Lower-court decision maker	Trial judge	Trial judge	Trial judge
Deference given to lower court	No deference	Substantial deference	Extreme deference
Party typically benefitted	Appellant	Appellee	Appellee
Definition	An appellate court reviews the legal question anew and independently, without regard to the conclusions reached by the trial court. "When *de novo* review is compelled, no form of appellate deference is acceptable." *Salve Regina College v. Russell*, (1991).	A finding is 'clearly erroneous' when although there is evidence to support it, the reviewing court on the entire evidence is left with the definite and firm conviction that a mistake has been committed. *United States v. United States Gypsum Co.*, (1948) "If the district court's account of the evidence is plausible in light of the record viewed in its entirety, the court of appeals may not reverse it even though convinced that had it been sitting as the trier of fact, it would have weighed the evidence differently. When there are two permissible views of the evidence, the factfinder's choice between them cannot be clearly erroneous." *Anderson v. Bessemer City*, (1985).	Generally, an abuse of discretion only occurs where no reasonable person could take the view adopted by the trial court. If reasonable persons could differ, no abuse of discretion can be found. *Harrington v. DeVito*, (7th Cir.1981) Under the abuse of discretion standard, a trial court's decision will not be disturbed unless the appellate court has a definite and firm conviction that the lower court made a clear error of judgment or exceeded the bounds of permissible choice in the circumstances. We will not alter a trial court's decision unless it can be shown that the court's decision was an arbitrary, capricious, whimsical, or manifestly unreasonable judgment. *Wright v. Abbott Laboratories, Inc.*, (10th Cir. 2001)
Examples	Motions for summary judgment, constitutional questions, statutory interpretation	Questions regarding who did what, where, and when; questions of intent and motive; questions of ultimate fact (such as negligence)	Rule 11 sanctions, attorney's fees, courtroom management, motions to compel, injunctions, and temporary restraining orders.

The Massachusetts Court System

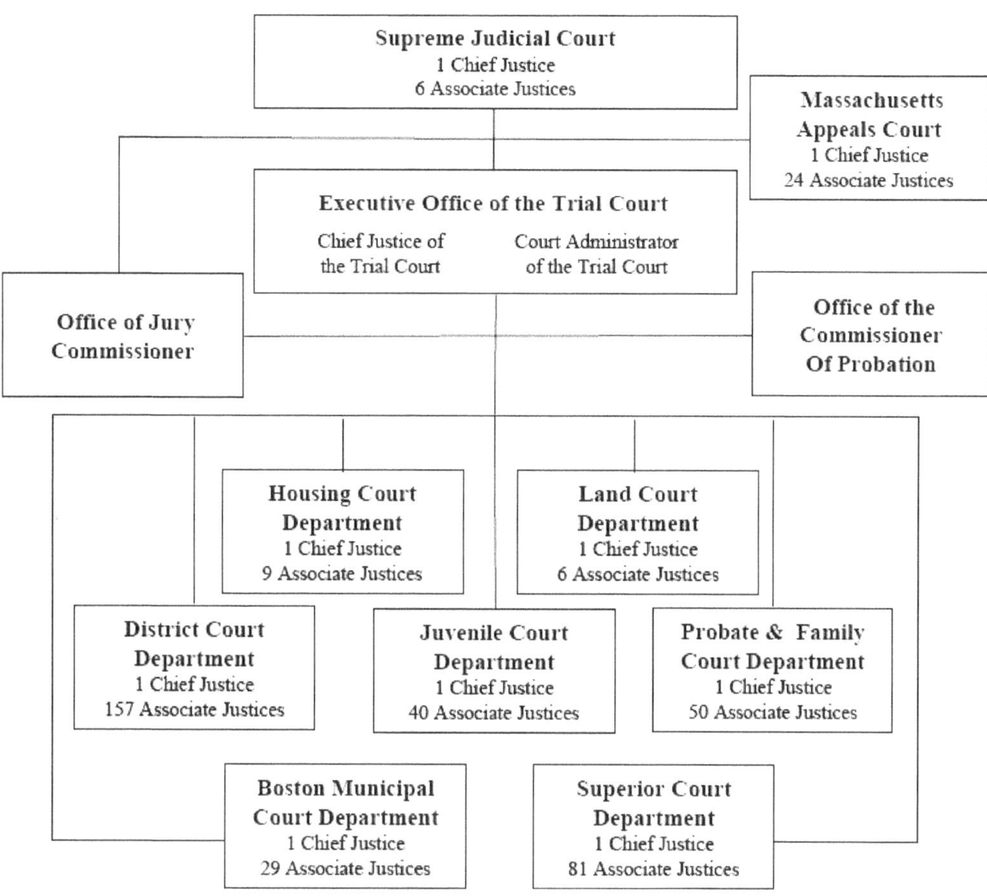

Notes for active learning

The Massachusetts Courts' Structure

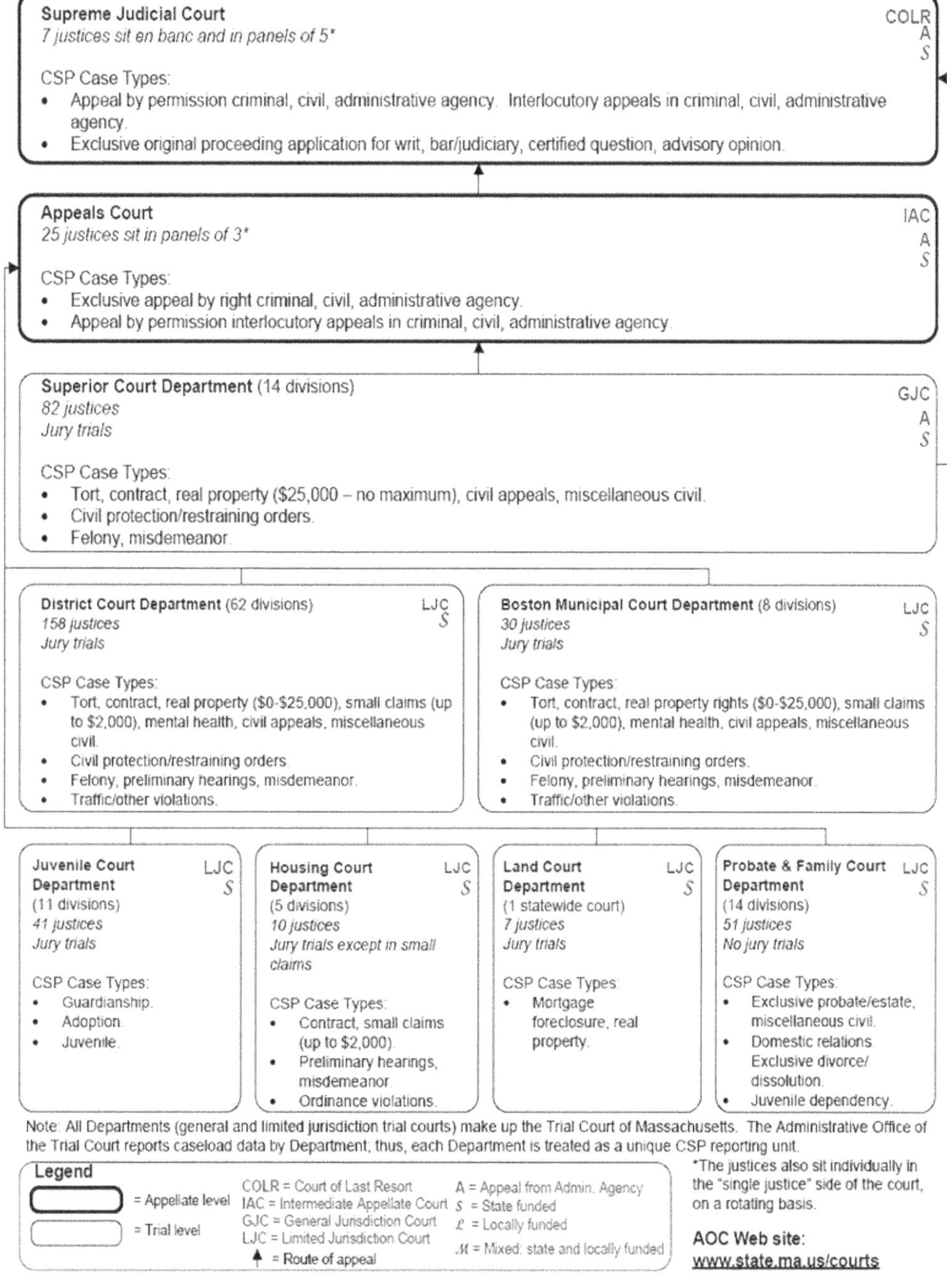

Notes for active learning

The New York Courts' Structure

Civil court structure

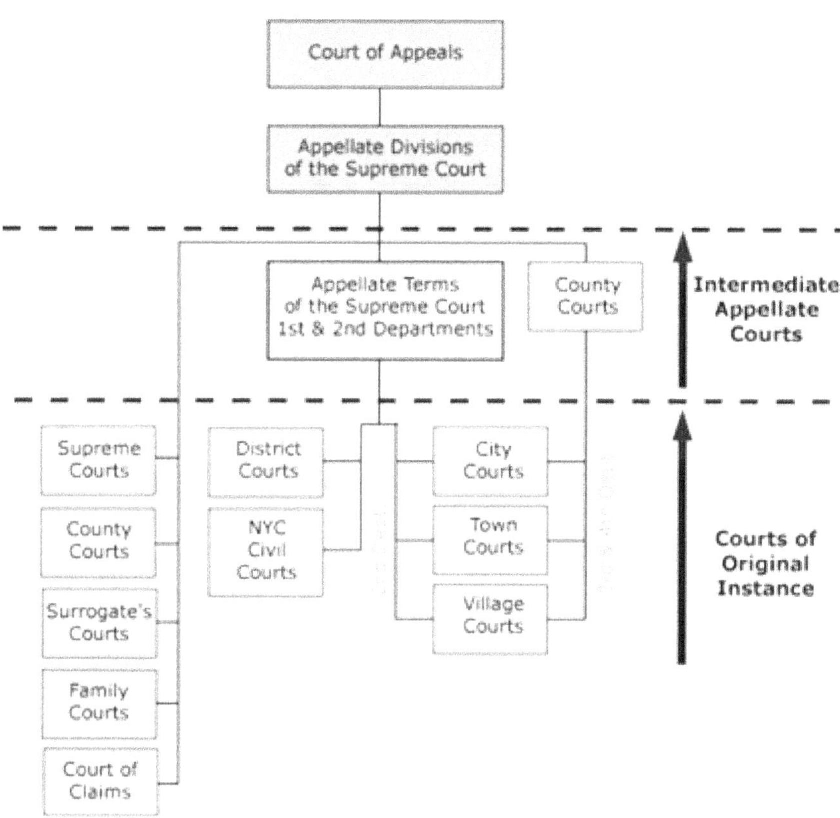

Criminal court structure

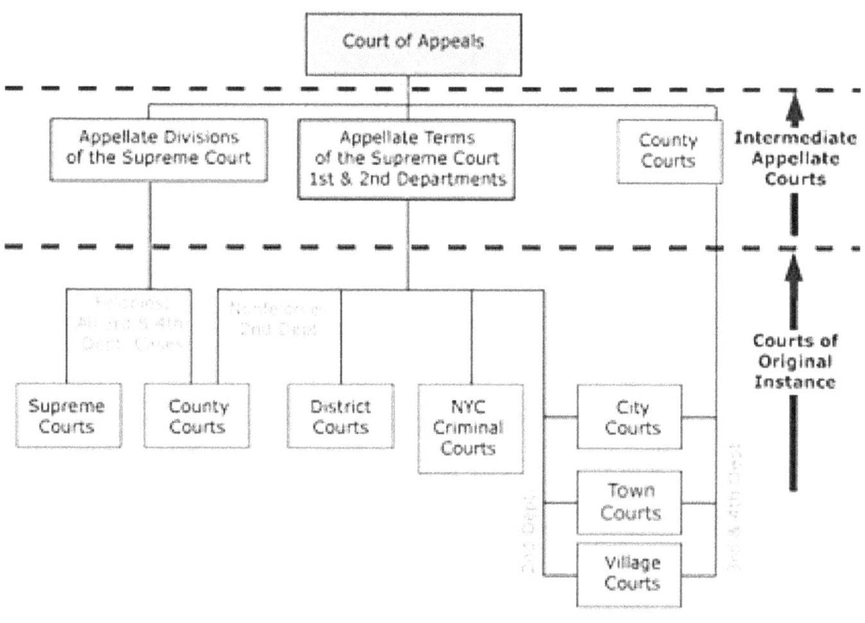

Notes for active learning

The Constitution of the United States (*a transcription*)

THE U.S. NATIONAL ARCHIVES & RECORDS ADMINISTRATION
www.archives.gov

The following text is a transcription of the Constitution as it was inscribed by Jacob Shallus on parchment (the document on display in the Rotunda at the National Archives Museum.) The spelling and punctuation reflect the original.

The Constitution of the United States: A Transcription

The following text is a transcription of the Constitution as it was inscribed by Jacob Shallus on parchment (displayed in the Rotunda at the National Archives Museum.) The authenticated text of the Constitution can be found on the website of the Government Printing Office.

We the People of the United States, in Order to form a more perfect Union, establish Justice, insure domestic Tranquility, provide for the common defence, promote the general Welfare, and secure the Blessings of Liberty to ourselves and our Posterity, do ordain and establish this Constitution for the United States of America.

Article. I

Section. 1.

All legislative Powers herein granted shall be vested in a Congress of the United States, which shall consist of a Senate and House of Representatives.

Section. 2.

The House of Representatives shall be composed of Members chosen every second Year by the People of the several States, and the Electors in each State shall have the Qualifications requisite for Electors of the most numerous Branch of the State Legislature.

No Person shall be a Representative who shall not have attained to the Age of twenty five Years, and been seven Years a Citizen of the United States, and who shall not, when elected, be an Inhabitant of that State in which he shall be chosen.

Representatives and direct Taxes shall be apportioned among the several States which may be included within this Union, according to their respective Numbers, which shall be determined by adding to the whole Number of free Persons, including those bound to Service for a Term of Years, and excluding Indians not taxed, three fifths of all other Persons. The actual Enumeration shall be made within three Years after the first Meeting of the Congress of the United States, and within every subsequent Term of ten Years, in such Manner as they shall by Law direct. The Number of Representatives shall not exceed one for every thirty Thousand, but each State shall have at Least one Representative; and until such enumeration shall be made, the State of New Hampshire shall be entitled to chuse three, Massachusetts eight, Rhode-Island and Providence

Plantations one, Connecticut five, New-York six, New Jersey four, Pennsylvania eight, Delaware one, Maryland six, Virginia ten, North Carolina five, South Carolina five, and Georgia three.

When vacancies happen in the Representation from any State, the Executive Authority thereof shall issue Writs of Election to fill such Vacancies.

The House of Representatives shall chuse their Speaker and other Officers; and shall have the sole Power of Impeachment.

Section. 3.

The Senate of the United States shall be composed of two Senators from each State, chosen by the Legislature thereof, for six Years; and each Senator shall have one Vote.

Immediately after they shall be assembled in Consequence of the first Election, they shall be divided as equally as may be into three Classes. The Seats of the Senators of the first Class shall be vacated at the Expiration of the second Year, of the second Class at the Expiration of the fourth Year, and of the third Class at the Expiration of the sixth Year, so that one third may be chosen every second Year; and if Vacancies happen by Resignation, or otherwise, during the Recess of the Legislature of any State, the Executive thereof may make temporary Appointments until the next Meeting of the Legislature, which shall then fill such Vacancies.

No Person shall be a Senator who shall not have attained to the Age of thirty Years, and been nine Years a Citizen of the United States, and who shall not, when elected, be an Inhabitant of that State for which he shall be chosen.

The Vice President of the United States shall be President of the Senate, but shall have no Vote, unless they be equally divided.

The Senate shall chuse their other Officers, and also a President pro tempore, in the Absence of the Vice President, or when he shall exercise the Office of President of the United States.

The Senate shall have the sole Power to try all Impeachments. When sitting for that Purpose, they shall be on Oath or Affirmation. When the President of the United States is tried, the Chief Justice shall preside: And no Person shall be convicted without the Concurrence of two thirds of the Members present.

Judgment in Cases of Impeachment shall not extend further than to removal from Office, and disqualification to hold and enjoy any Office of honor, Trust or Profit under the United States: but the Party convicted shall nevertheless be liable and subject to Indictment, Trial, Judgment and Punishment, according to Law.

Section. 4.

The Times, Places and Manner of holding Elections for Senators and Representatives, shall be prescribed in each State by the Legislature thereof; but the Congress may at any time by Law make or alter such Regulations, except as to the Places of chusing Senators.

The Congress shall assemble at least once in every Year, and such Meeting shall be on the first Monday in December, unless they shall by Law appoint a different Day.

Section. 5.

Each House shall be the Judge of the Elections, Returns and Qualifications of its own Members, and a Majority of each shall constitute a Quorum to do Business; but a smaller Number may adjourn from day to day, and may be authorized to compel the Attendance of absent Members, in such Manner, and under such Penalties as each House may provide.

Each House may determine the Rules of its Proceedings, punish its Members for disorderly Behaviour, and, with the Concurrence of two thirds, expel a Member.

Each House shall keep a Journal of its Proceedings, and from time to time publish the same, excepting such Parts as may in their Judgment require Secrecy; and the Yeas and Nays of the Members of either House on any question shall, at the Desire of one fifth of those Present, be entered on the Journal.

Neither House, during the Session of Congress, shall, without the Consent of the other, adjourn for more than three days, nor to any other Place than that in which the two Houses shall be sitting.

Section. 6.

The Senators and Representatives shall receive a Compensation for their Services, to be ascertained by Law, and paid out of the Treasury of the United States. They shall in all Cases, except Treason, Felony and Breach of the Peace, be privileged from Arrest during their Attendance at the Session of their respective Houses, and in going to and returning from the same; and for any Speech or Debate in either House, they shall not be questioned in any other Place.

No Senator or Representative shall, during the Time for which he was elected, be appointed to any civil Office under the Authority of the United States, which shall have been created, or the Emoluments whereof shall have been encreased during such time; and no Person holding any Office under the United States, shall be a Member of either House during his Continuance in Office.

Section. 7.

All Bills for raising Revenue shall originate in the House of Representatives; but the Senate may propose or concur with Amendments as on other Bills.

Every Bill which shall have passed the House of Representatives and the Senate, shall, before it become a Law, be presented to the President of the United States; If he approves he shall sign it, but if not he shall return it, with his Objections to that House in which it shall have originated, who shall enter the Objections at large on their Journal, and proceed to reconsider it. If after such Reconsideration two thirds of that House shall agree to pass the Bill, it shall be sent, together with the Objections, to the other House, by which it shall likewise be reconsidered, and if approved by two thirds of that House, it shall become a Law. But in all such Cases the Votes of both Houses shall be determined by yeas and Nays, and the Names of the Persons voting for and against the Bill shall be entered on the Journal of each House respectively. If any Bill shall not be returned by the President within ten Days (Sundays excepted) after it shall have been presented to him, the Same shall be a Law, in like Manner as if he had signed it, unless the Congress by their Adjournment prevent its Return, in which Case it shall not be a Law.

Every Order, Resolution, or Vote to which the Concurrence of the Senate and House of Representatives may be necessary (except on a question of Adjournment) shall be presented to the President of the United States; and before the Same shall take Effect, shall be approved by him, or being disapproved by him, shall be repassed by two thirds of the Senate and House of Representatives, according to the Rules and Limitations prescribed in the Case of a Bill.

Section. 8.

The Congress shall have Power To lay and collect Taxes, Duties, Imposts and Excises, to pay the Debts and provide for the common Defence and general Welfare of the United States; but all Duties, Imposts and Excises shall be uniform throughout the United States;

To borrow Money on the credit of the United States;

To regulate Commerce with foreign Nations, and among the several States, and with the Indian Tribes;

To establish an uniform Rule of Naturalization, and uniform Laws on the subject of Bankruptcies throughout the United States;

To coin Money, regulate the Value thereof, and of foreign Coin, and fix the Standard of Weights and Measures;

To provide for the Punishment of counterfeiting the Securities and current Coin of the United States;

To establish Post Offices and post Roads;

To promote the Progress of Science and useful Arts, by securing for limited Times to Authors and Inventors the exclusive Right to their respective Writings and Discoveries;

To constitute Tribunals inferior to the Supreme Court;

To define and punish Piracies and Felonies committed on the high Seas, and Offences against the Law of Nations;

To declare War, grant Letters of Marque and Reprisal, and make Rules concerning Captures on Land and Water;

To raise and support Armies, but no Appropriation of Money to that Use shall be for a longer Term than two Years;

To provide and maintain a Navy;

To make Rules for the Government and Regulation of the land and naval Forces;

To provide for calling forth the Militia to execute the Laws of the Union, suppress Insurrections and repel Invasions;

To provide for organizing, arming, and disciplining, the Militia, and for governing such Part of them as may be employed in the Service of the United States, reserving to the States respectively, the Appointment of the Officers, and the Authority of training the Militia according to the discipline prescribed by Congress;

To exercise exclusive Legislation in all Cases whatsoever, over such District (not exceeding ten Miles square) as may, by Cession of particular States, and the Acceptance of Congress, become the Seat of the Government of the United States, and to exercise like Authority over all Places purchased by the Consent of the Legislature of the State in which the Same shall be, for the Erection of Forts, Magazines, Arsenals, dock-Yards, and other needful Buildings;—And

To make all Laws which shall be necessary and proper for carrying into Execution the foregoing Powers, and all other Powers vested by this Constitution in the Government of the United States, or in any Department or Officer thereof.

Section. 9.

The Migration or Importation of such Persons as any of the States now existing shall think proper to admit, shall not be prohibited by the Congress prior to the Year one thousand eight hundred and eight, but a Tax or duty may be imposed on such Importation, not exceeding ten dollars for each Person.

The Privilege of the Writ of Habeas Corpus shall not be suspended, unless when in Cases of Rebellion or Invasion the public Safety may require it.

No Bill of Attainder or ex post facto Law shall be passed.

No Capitation, or other direct, Tax shall be laid, unless in Proportion to the Census or enumeration herein before directed to be taken.

No Tax or Duty shall be laid on Articles exported from any State.

No Preference shall be given by any Regulation of Commerce or Revenue to the Ports of one State over those of another: nor shall Vessels bound to, or from, one State, be obliged to enter, clear, or pay Duties in another.

No Money shall be drawn from the Treasury, but in Consequence of Appropriations made by Law; and a regular Statement and Account of the Receipts and Expenditures of all public Money shall be published from time to time.

No Title of Nobility shall be granted by the United States: And no Person holding any Office of Profit or Trust under them, shall, without the Consent of the Congress, accept of any present, Emolument, Office, or Title, of any kind whatever, from any King, Prince, or foreign State.

Section. 10.

No State shall enter into any Treaty, Alliance, or Confederation; grant Letters of Marque and Reprisal; coin Money; emit Bills of Credit; make any Thing but gold and silver Coin a Tender in Payment of Debts; pass any Bill of Attainder, ex post facto Law, or Law impairing the Obligation of Contracts, or grant any Title of Nobility.

No State shall, without the Consent of the Congress, lay any Imposts or Duties on Imports or Exports, except what may be absolutely necessary for executing it's inspection Laws: and the net

Produce of all Duties and Imposts, laid by any State on Imports or Exports, shall be for the Use of the Treasury of the United States; and all such Laws shall be subject to the Revision and Controul of the Congress.

No State shall, without the Consent of Congress, lay any Duty of Tonnage, keep Troops, or Ships of War in time of Peace, enter into any Agreement or Compact with another State, or with a foreign Power, or engage in War, unless actually invaded, or in such imminent Danger as will not admit of delay.

Article. II

Section. 1.

The executive Power shall be vested in a President of the United States of America. He shall hold his Office during the Term of four Years, and, together with the Vice President, chosen for the same Term, be elected, as follows

Each State shall appoint, in such Manner as the Legislature thereof may direct, a Number of Electors, equal to the whole Number of Senators and Representatives to which the State may be entitled in the Congress: but no Senator or Representative, or Person holding an Office of Trust or Profit under the United States, shall be appointed an Elector.

The Electors shall meet in their respective States, and vote by Ballot for two Persons, of whom one at least shall not be an Inhabitant of the same State with themselves. And they shall make a List of all the Persons voted for, and of the Number of Votes for each; which List they shall sign and certify, and transmit sealed to the Seat of the Government of the United States, directed to the President of the Senate. The President of the Senate shall, in the Presence of the Senate and House of Representatives, open all the Certificates, and the Votes shall then be counted. The Person having the greatest Number of Votes shall be the President, if such Number be a Majority of the whole Number of Electors appointed; and if there be more than one who have such Majority, and have an equal Number of Votes, then the House of Representatives shall immediately chuse by Ballot one of them for President; and if no Person have a Majority, then from the five highest on the List the said House shall in like Manner chuse the President. But in chusing the President, the Votes shall be taken by States, the Representation from each State having one Vote; A quorum for this Purpose shall consist of a Member or Members from two thirds of the States, and a Majority of all the States shall be necessary to a Choice. In every Case, after the Choice of the President, the Person having the greatest Number of Votes of the Electors shall be the Vice President. But if there should remain two or more who have equal Votes, the Senate shall chuse from them by Ballot the Vice President.

The Congress may determine the Time of chusing the Electors, and the Day on which they shall give their Votes; which Day shall be the same throughout the United States.

No Person except a natural born Citizen, or a Citizen of the United States, at the time of the Adoption of this Constitution, shall be eligible to the Office of President; neither shall any Person be eligible to that Office who shall not have attained to the Age of thirty five Years, and been fourteen Years a Resident within the United States.

In Case of the Removal of the President from Office, or of his Death, Resignation, or Inability to discharge the Powers and Duties of the said Office, the Same shall devolve on the Vice President, and the Congress may by Law provide for the Case of Removal, Death, Resignation or Inability, both of the President and Vice President, declaring what Officer shall then act as President, and such Officer shall act accordingly, until the Disability be removed, or a President shall be elected.

The President shall, at stated Times, receive for his Services, a Compensation, which shall neither be encreased nor diminished during the Period for which he shall have been elected, and he shall not receive within that Period any other Emolument from the United States, or any of them.

Before he enters on the Execution of his Office, he shall take the following Oath or Affirmation:—"I do solemnly swear (or affirm) that I will faithfully execute the Office of President of the United States, and will to the best of my Ability, preserve, protect and defend the Constitution of the United States."

Section. 2.

The President shall be Commander in Chief of the Army and Navy of the United States, and of the Militia of the several States, when called into the actual Service of the United States; he may require the Opinion, in writing, of the principal Officer in each of the executive Departments, upon any Subject relating to the Duties of their respective Offices, and he shall have Power to grant Reprieves and Pardons for Offences against the United States, except in Cases of Impeachment.

He shall have Power, by and with the Advice and Consent of the Senate, to make Treaties, provided two thirds of the Senators present concur; and he shall nominate, and by and with the Advice and Consent of the Senate, shall appoint Ambassadors, other public Ministers and Consuls, Judges of the supreme Court, and all other Officers of the United States, whose Appointments are not herein otherwise provided for, and which shall be established by Law: but the Congress may by Law vest the Appointment of such inferior Officers, as they think proper, in the President alone, in the Courts of Law, or in the Heads of Departments.

The President shall have Power to fill up all Vacancies that may happen during the Recess of the Senate, by granting Commissions which shall expire at the End of their next Session.

Section. 3.

He shall from time to time give to the Congress Information of the State of the Union, and recommend to their Consideration such Measures as he shall judge necessary and expedient; he may, on extraordinary Occasions, convene both Houses, or either of them, and in Case of Disagreement between them, with Respect to the Time of Adjournment, he may adjourn them to such Time as he shall think proper; he shall receive Ambassadors and other public Ministers; he shall take Care that the Laws be faithfully executed, and shall Commission all the Officers of the United States.

Section. 4.

The President, Vice President and all civil Officers of the United States, shall be removed from Office on Impeachment for, and Conviction of, Treason, Bribery, or other high Crimes and Misdemeanors.

Article III

Section. 1.

The judicial Power of the United States, shall be vested in one supreme Court, and in such inferior Courts as the Congress may from time to time ordain and establish. The Judges, both of the supreme and inferior Courts, shall hold their Offices during good Behaviour, and shall, at stated Times, receive for their Services, a Compensation, which shall not be diminished during their Continuance in Office.

Section. 2.

The judicial Power shall extend to all Cases, in Law and Equity, arising under this Constitution, the Laws of the United States, and Treaties made, or which shall be made, under their Authority;— to all Cases affecting Ambassadors, other public Ministers and Consuls;—to all Cases of admiralty and maritime Jurisdiction;—to Controversies to which the United States shall be a Party;—to Controversies between two or more States;—between a State and Citizens of another State,— between Citizens of different States,—between Citizens of the same State claiming Lands under Grants of different States, and between a State, or the Citizens thereof, and foreign States, Citizens or Subjects.

In all Cases affecting Ambassadors, other public Ministers and Consuls, and those in which a State shall be Party, the supreme Court shall have original Jurisdiction. In all the other Cases before mentioned, the supreme Court shall have appellate Jurisdiction, both as to Law and Fact, with such Exceptions, and under such Regulations as the Congress shall make.

The Trial of all Crimes, except in Cases of Impeachment, shall be by Jury; and such Trial shall be held in the State where the said Crimes shall have been committed; but when not committed within any State, the Trial shall be at such Place or Places as the Congress may by Law have directed.

Section. 3.

Treason against the United States, shall consist only in levying War against them, or in adhering to their Enemies, giving them Aid and Comfort. No Person shall be convicted of Treason unless on the Testimony of two Witnesses to the same overt Act, or on Confession in open Court.

The Congress shall have Power to declare the Punishment of Treason, but no Attainder of Treason shall work Corruption of Blood, or Forfeiture except during the Life of the Person attainted.

Article. IV

Section. 1.

Full Faith and Credit shall be given in each State to the public Acts, Records, and judicial Proceedings of every other State. And the Congress may by general Laws prescribe the Manner in which such Acts, Records and Proceedings shall be proved, and the Effect thereof.

Section. 2.

The Citizens of each State shall be entitled to all Privileges and Immunities of Citizens in the several States.

A Person charged in any State with Treason, Felony, or other Crime, who shall flee from Justice, and be found in another State, shall on Demand of the executive Authority of the State from which he fled, be delivered up, to be removed to the State having Jurisdiction of the Crime.

No Person held to Service or Labour in one State, under the Laws thereof, escaping into another, shall, in Consequence of any Law or Regulation therein, be discharged from such Service or Labour, but shall be delivered up on Claim of the Party to whom such Service or Labour may be due.

Section. 3.

New States may be admitted by the Congress into this Union; but no new State shall be formed or erected within the Jurisdiction of any other State; nor any State be formed by the Junction of two or more States, or Parts of States, without the Consent of the Legislatures of the States concerned as well as of the Congress.

The Congress shall have Power to dispose of and make all needful Rules and Regulations respecting the Territory or other Property belonging to the United States; and nothing in this Constitution shall be so construed as to Prejudice any Claims of the United States, or of any particular State.

Section. 4.

The United States shall guarantee to every State in this Union a Republican Form of Government, and shall protect each of them against Invasion; and on Application of the Legislature, or of the Executive (when the Legislature cannot be convened), against domestic Violence.

Article. V

The Congress, whenever two thirds of both Houses shall deem it necessary, shall propose Amendments to this Constitution, or, on the Application of the Legislatures of two thirds of the several States, shall call a Convention for proposing Amendments, which, in either Case, shall be valid to all Intents and Purposes, as Part of this Constitution, when ratified by the Legislatures of three fourths of the several States, or by Conventions in three fourths thereof, as the one or the other Mode of Ratification may be proposed by the Congress; Provided that no Amendment which may be made prior to the Year One thousand eight hundred and eight shall in any Manner affect the first and fourth Clauses in the Ninth Section of the first Article; and that no State, without its Consent, shall be deprived of its equal Suffrage in the Senate.

Article. VI

All Debts contracted and Engagements entered into, before the Adoption of this Constitution, shall be as valid against the United States under this Constitution, as under the Confederation.

This Constitution, and the Laws of the United States which shall be made in Pursuance thereof; and all Treaties made, or which shall be made, under the Authority of the United States, shall be the supreme Law of the Land; and the Judges in every State shall be bound thereby, any Thing in the Constitution or Laws of any State to the Contrary notwithstanding.

The Senators and Representatives before mentioned, and the Members of the several State Legislatures, and all executive and judicial Officers, both of the United States and of the several States, shall be bound by Oath or Affirmation, to support this Constitution; but no religious Test shall ever be required as a Qualification to any Office or public Trust under the United States.

Article. VII

The Ratification of the Conventions of nine States, shall be sufficient for the Establishment of this Constitution between the States so ratifying the Same.

The Word, "the," being interlined between the seventh and eighth Lines of the first Page, The Word "Thirty" being partly written on an Erazure in the fifteenth Line of the first Page, The Words "is tried" being interlined between the thirty second and thirty third Lines of the first Page and the Word "the" being interlined between the forty third and forty fourth Lines of the second Page.

Attest William Jackson Secretary, done in Convention by the Unanimous Consent of the States present the Seventeenth Day of September in the Year of our Lord one thousand seven hundred and Eighty seven and of the Independance of the United States of America the Twelfth In witness whereof We have hereunto subscribed our Names, G°. Washington, *Presidt and deputy from Virginia*

Delaware
Geo: Read
Gunning Bedford jun
John Dickinson
Richard Bassett
Jaco: Broom

Maryland
James McHenry
Dan of St Thos.
Jenifer
Danl. Carroll

Virginia
John Blair
James Madison Jr.

North Carolina
Wm. Blount
Richd. Dobbs
Spaight
Hu Williamson

South Carolina
J. Rutledge
Charles Cotesworth
Pinckney
Charles Pinckney
Pierce Butler

Georgia
William Few
Abr Baldwin

New Hampshire
John Langdon
Nicholas Gilman

Massachusetts
Nathaniel Gorham
Rufus King

Connecticut
Wm. Saml. Johnson
Roger Sherman

New York
Alexander Hamilton

New Jersey
Wil: Livingston
David Brearley
Wm. Paterson
Jona: Dayton

Pensylvania
B Franklin
Thomas Mifflin
Robt. Morris
Geo. Clymer
Thos. FitzSimons
Jared Ingersoll
James Wilson
Gouv Morris

Enactment of the Bill of Rights of the United States of America (1791)

The first ten Amendments to the Constitution make up the Bill of Rights. Written by James Madison in response to calls from several states for greater constitutional protection for individual liberties, the Bill of Rights lists specific prohibitions on governmental power. The Virginia Declaration of Rights, written by George Mason, strongly influenced Madison.

One of the contention points between Federalists and Anti-Federalists was the Constitution's lack of a bill of rights that would place specific limits on government power.

Federalists argued that the Constitution did not need a bill of rights because the people and the states kept powers not explicitly given to the federal government.

Anti-Federalists held that a *bill of rights* was necessary to safeguard individual liberty.

Madison, then a member of the U.S. House of Representatives, went through the Constitution itself, making changes where he thought most appropriate.

Several Representatives, led by Roger Sherman, objected that Congress had no authority to change the wording of the Constitution. Therefore, Madison's changes were presented as a list of amendments that would follow Article VII.

The House approved 17 amendments. Of these 17, the Senate approved 12. Those 12 were sent to the states for approval in August of 1789. Of those 12 proposed amendments, 10 were quickly ratified. Virginia's legislature became the last to ratify the Amendments on December 15, 1791. These Amendments are the Bill of Rights.

The Bill of Rights is a list of limits on government power. For example, what the Founders saw as the natural right of individuals to speak and worship freely was protected by the First Amendment's prohibitions on Congress from making laws establishing a religion or abridging freedom of speech.

Another example is the natural right to be free from the government's unreasonable intrusion in one's home was safeguarded by the Fourth Amendment's warrant requirements.

Other precursors to the Bill of Rights include English documents such as the Magna Carta[1], the Petition of Rights, the English Bill of Rights, and the Massachusetts Body of Liberties.

The Magna Carta illustrates Compact Theory[1] as well as initial strides toward limited government. Its provisions address individual rights and political rights. Latin for "Great Charter," the Magna Carta was written by Barons in Runnymede, England, and forced on the King.

Although the protections were generally limited to the prerogatives of the Barons, the Magna Carta embodied the general principle that the King accepted limitations on his rule. These included the fundamental acknowledgment that the king was not above the law.

Included in the Magna Carta are protections for the English church, petitioning the king, freedom from the forced quarter of troops and unreasonable searches, due process and fair trial

---

protections, and freedom from excessive fines. These protections can be found in the First, Third, Fourth, Fifth, Sixth, and Eighth Amendments to the Constitution.

The Magna Carta is the oldest compact in England. The Mayflower Compact, the Fundamental Orders of Connecticut, and the Albany Plan are examples from the American colonies.

The Articles of Confederation was a compact among the states, and the Constitution creates a compact based on a federal system between the national government, state governments, and the people. The Hayne-Webster Debate focused on the compact created by the Constitution.

[1] Philosophers including Thomas Hobbes, John Locke, and Jean-Jacques Rousseau theorized that peoples' condition in a "state of nature" (that is, outside of society) is one of freedom, but that freedom inevitably degrades into war, chaos, or debilitating competition without the benefit of a system of laws and government. They reasoned, therefore, that for their happiness, individuals willingly trade some of their natural freedom in exchange for the protections provided by the government.

The Bill of Rights: Amendments I–X

Amendment I

Congress shall make no law respecting an establishment of religion, or prohibiting the free exercise thereof; or abridging the freedom of speech, or of the press; or the right of the people peaceably to assemble, and to petition the government for a redress of grievances.

Amendment II

A well regulated militia, being necessary to the security of a free state, the right of the people to keep and bear arms, shall not be infringed.

Amendment III

No soldier shall, in time of peace be quartered in any house, without the consent of the owner, nor in time of war, but in a manner to be prescribed by law.

Amendment IV

The right of the people to be secure in their persons, houses, papers, and effects, against unreasonable searches and seizures, shall not be violated, and no warrants shall issue, but upon probable cause, supported by oath or affirmation, and particularly describing the place to be searched, and the persons or things to be seized.

Amendment V

No person shall be held to answer for a capital, or otherwise infamous crime, unless on a presentment or indictment of a grand jury, except in cases arising in the land or naval forces, or in the militia, when in actual service in time of war or public danger; nor shall any person be subject for the same offense to be twice put in jeopardy of life or limb; nor shall be compelled in any criminal case to be a witness against himself, nor be deprived of life, liberty, or property, without due process of law; nor shall private property be taken for public use, without just compensation.

Amendment VI

In all criminal prosecutions, the accused shall enjoy the right to a speedy and public trial, by an impartial jury of the state and district wherein the crime shall have been committed, which district shall have been previously ascertained by law, and to be informed of the nature and cause of the accusation; to be confronted with the witnesses against him; to have compulsory process for obtaining witnesses in his favor, and to have the assistance of counsel for his defense.

Amendment VII

In suits at common law, where the value in controversy shall exceed twenty dollars, the right of trial by jury shall be preserved, and no fact tried by a jury, shall be otherwise reexamined in any court of the United States, than according to the rules of the common law.

Amendment VIII

Excessive bail shall not be required, nor excessive fines imposed, nor cruel and unusual punishments inflicted.

Amendment IX

The enumeration in the Constitution, of certain rights, shall not be construed to deny or disparage others retained by the people.

Amendment X

The powers not delegated to the United States by the Constitution, nor prohibited by it to the states, are reserved to the states respectively, or to the people.

Constitutional Amendments XI–XXVII

AMENDMENT XI

Passed by Congress March 4, 1794. Ratified February 7, 1795.

Note: Article III, section 2, of the Constitution was modified by amendment 11.

The Judicial power of the United States shall not be construed to extend to any suit in law or equity, commenced or prosecuted against one of the United States by Citizens of another State, or by Citizens or Subjects of any Foreign State.

AMENDMENT XII

Passed by Congress December 9, 1803. Ratified June 15, 1804.

Note: A portion of Article II, section 1 of the Constitution was superseded by the 12th amendment.

The Electors shall meet in their respective states and vote by ballot for President and Vice-President, one of whom, at least, shall not be an inhabitant of the same state with themselves; they shall name in their ballots the person voted for as President, and in distinct ballots the person voted for as Vice-President, and they shall make distinct lists of all persons voted for as President, and of all persons voted for as Vice-President, and of the number of votes for each, which lists they shall sign and certify, and transmit sealed to the seat of the government of the United States, directed to the President of the Senate; -- the President of the Senate shall, in the presence of the Senate and House of Representatives, open all the certificates and the votes shall then be counted; -- The person having the greatest number of votes for President, shall be the President, if such number be a majority of the whole number of Electors appointed; and if no person have such majority, then from the persons having the highest numbers not exceeding three on the list of those voted for as President, the House of Representatives shall choose immediately, by ballot, the President. But in choosing the President, the votes shall be taken by states, the representation from each state having one vote; a quorum for this purpose shall consist of a member or members from two-thirds of the states, and a majority of all the states shall be necessary to a choice. [And if the House of Representatives shall not choose a President whenever the right of choice shall devolve upon them, before the fourth day of March next following, then the Vice-President shall act as President, as in case of the death or other constitutional disability of the President. --]* The person having the greatest number of votes as Vice-President, shall be the Vice-President, if such number be a majority of the whole number of Electors appointed, and if no person have a majority, then from the two highest numbers on the list, the Senate shall choose the Vice-President; a quorum for the purpose shall consist of two-thirds of the whole number of Senators, and a majority of the whole number shall be necessary to a choice. But no person constitutionally ineligible to the office of President shall be eligible to that of Vice-President of the United States.

**Superseded by section 3 of the 20th Amendment.*

AMENDMENT XIII

Passed by Congress January 31, 1865. Ratified December 6, 1865.

Note: A portion of Article IV, section 2, of the Constitution was superseded by the 13th amendment.

Section 1.

Neither slavery nor involuntary servitude, except as a punishment for crime whereof the party shall have been duly convicted, shall exist within the United States, or any place subject to their jurisdiction.

Section 2.

Congress shall have power to enforce this article by appropriate legislation.

AMENDMENT XIV

Passed by Congress June 13, 1866. Ratified July 9, 1868.

Note: Article I, section 2, of the Constitution was modified by section 2 of the 14th amendment.

Section 1.

All persons born or naturalized in the United States, and subject to the jurisdiction thereof, are citizens of the United States and of the State wherein they reside. No State shall make or enforce any law which shall abridge the privileges or immunities of citizens of the United States; nor shall any State deprive any person of life, liberty, or property, without due process of law; nor deny to any person within its jurisdiction the equal protection of the laws.

Section 2.

Representatives shall be apportioned among the several States according to their respective numbers, counting the whole number of persons in each State, excluding Indians not taxed. But when the right to vote at any election for the choice of electors for President and Vice-President of the United States, Representatives in Congress, the Executive and Judicial officers of a State, or the members of the Legislature thereof, is denied to any of the male inhabitants of such State, being twenty-one years of age,* and citizens of the United States, or in any way abridged, except for participation in rebellion, or other crime, the basis of representation therein shall be reduced in the proportion which the number of such male citizens shall bear to the whole number of male citizens twenty-one years of age in such State.

Section 3.

No person shall be a Senator or Representative in Congress, or elector of President and Vice-President, or hold any office, civil or military, under the United States, or under any State, who, having previously taken an oath, as a member of Congress, or as an officer of the United States, or as a member of any State legislature, or as an executive or judicial officer of any State, to support the Constitution of the United States, shall have engaged in insurrection or rebellion against the same, or given aid or comfort to the enemies thereof. But Congress may by a vote of two-thirds of each House, remove such disability.

Section 4.

The validity of the public debt of the United States, authorized by law, including debts incurred for payment of pensions and bounties for services in suppressing insurrection or rebellion, shall not be questioned. But neither the United States nor any State shall assume or pay any debt or obligation incurred in aid of insurrection or rebellion against the United States, or any claim for the loss or emancipation of any slave; but all such debts, obligations and claims shall be held illegal and void.

Section 5.

The Congress shall have the power to enforce, by appropriate legislation, the provisions of this article.

**Changed by section 1 of the 26th Amendment.*

AMENDMENT XV

Passed by Congress February 26, 1869. Ratified February 3, 1870.

Section 1.

The right of citizens of the United States to vote shall not be denied or abridged by the United States or by any State on account of race, color, or previous condition of servitude.

Section 2.

The Congress shall have the power to enforce this article by appropriate legislation.

AMENDMENT XVI

Passed by Congress July 2, 1909. Ratified February 3, 1913.

Note: Article I, section 9, of the Constitution was modified by amendment 16.

The Congress shall have power to lay and collect taxes on incomes, from whatever source derived, without apportionment among the several States, and without regard to any census or enumeration.

AMENDMENT XVII

Passed by Congress May 13, 1912. Ratified April 8, 1913.

Note: Article I, section 3, of the Constitution was modified by the 17th Amendment.

The Senate of the United States shall be composed of two Senators from each State, elected by the people thereof, for six years; and each Senator shall have one vote. The electors in each State shall have the qualifications requisite for electors of the most numerous branch of the State legislatures.

When vacancies happen in the representation of any State in the Senate, the executive authority of such State shall issue writs of election to fill such vacancies: *Provided*, That the legislature of any State may empower the executive thereof to make temporary appointments until the people fill the vacancies by election as the legislature may direct.

This amendment shall not be so construed as to affect the election or term of any Senator chosen before it becomes valid as part of the Constitution.

AMENDMENT XVIII

Passed by Congress December 18, 1917. Ratified January 16, 1919. Repealed by Amendment 21.

Section 1.

After one year from the ratification of this article the manufacture, sale, or transportation of intoxicating liquors within, the importation thereof into, or the exportation thereof from the United States and all territory subject to the jurisdiction thereof for beverage purposes is hereby prohibited.

Section 2.

The Congress and the several States shall have concurrent power to enforce this article by appropriate legislation.

Section 3.

This article shall be inoperative unless it shall have been ratified as an amendment to the Constitution by the legislatures of the several States, as provided in the Constitution, within seven years from the date of the submission hereof to the States by the Congress.

AMENDMENT XIX

Passed by Congress June 4, 1919. Ratified August 18, 1920.

The right of citizens of the United States to vote shall not be denied or abridged by the United States or by any State on account of sex.

Congress shall have power to enforce this article by appropriate legislation.

AMENDMENT XX

Passed by Congress March 2, 1932. Ratified January 23, 1933.

Note: Article I, section 4, of the Constitution was modified by section 2 of this Amendment. In addition, a portion of the 12th Amendment was superseded by section 3.

Section 1.

The terms of the President and the Vice President shall end at noon on the 20th day of January, and the terms of Senators and Representatives at noon on the 3d day of January, of the years in which such terms would have ended if this article had not been ratified; and the terms of their successors shall then begin.

Section 2.

The Congress shall assemble at least once in every year, and such meeting shall begin at noon on the 3d day of January, unless they shall by law appoint a different day.

Section 3.

If, at the time fixed for the beginning of the term of the President, the President elect shall have died, the Vice President elect shall become President. If a President shall not have been chosen before the time fixed for the beginning of his term, or if the President elect shall have failed to qualify, then the Vice President elect shall act as President until a President shall have qualified; and the Congress may by law provide for the case wherein neither a President elect nor a Vice President elect shall have qualified, declaring who shall then act as President, or the manner in which one who is to act shall be selected, and such person shall act accordingly until a President or Vice President shall have qualified.

Section 4.

The Congress may by law provide for the case of the death of any of the persons from whom the House of Representatives may choose a President whenever the right of choice shall have devolved upon them, and for the case of the death of any of the persons from whom the Senate may choose a Vice President whenever the right of choice shall have devolved upon them.

Section 5.

Sections 1 and 2 shall take effect on the 15th day of October following the ratification of this article.

Section 6.

This article shall be inoperative unless it shall have been ratified as an amendment to the Constitution by the legislatures of three-fourths of the several States within seven years from the date of its submission.

AMENDMENT XXI

Passed by Congress February 20, 1933. Ratified December 5, 1933.

Section 1.

The eighteenth article of amendment to the Constitution of the United States is hereby repealed.

Section 2.

The transportation or importation into any State, Territory, or possession of the United States for delivery or use therein of intoxicating liquors, in violation of the laws thereof, is hereby prohibited.

Section 3.

This article shall be inoperative unless it shall have been ratified as an amendment to the Constitution by conventions in the several States, as provided in the Constitution, within seven years from the date of the submission hereof to the States by the Congress.

AMENDMENT XXII

Passed by Congress March 21, 1947. Ratified February 27, 1951.

Section 1.

No person shall be elected to the office of the President more than twice, and no person who has held the office of President, or acted as President, for more than two years of a term to which some other person was elected President shall be elected to the office of the President more than once. But this Article shall not apply to any person holding the office of President when this Article was proposed by the Congress, and shall not prevent any person who may be holding the office of President, or acting as President, during the term within which this Article becomes operative from holding the office of President or acting as President during the remainder of such term.

Section 2.

This article shall be inoperative unless it shall have been ratified as an amendment to the Constitution by the legislatures of three-fourths of the several States within seven years from the date of its submission to the States by the Congress.

AMENDMENT XXIII

Passed by Congress June 16, 1960. Ratified March 29, 1961.

Section 1.

The District constituting the seat of Government of the United States shall appoint in such manner as the Congress may direct:

A number of electors of President and Vice President equal to the whole number of Senators and Representatives in Congress to which the District would be entitled if it were a State, but in no event more than the least populous State; they shall be in addition to those appointed by the States, but they shall be considered, for the purposes of the election of President and Vice President, to be electors appointed by a State; and they shall meet in the District and perform such duties as provided by the twelfth article of amendment.

Section 2.

The Congress shall have power to enforce this article by appropriate legislation.

AMENDMENT XXIV

Passed by Congress August 27, 1962. Ratified January 23, 1964.

Section 1.

The right of citizens of the United States to vote in any primary or other election for President or Vice President, for electors for President or Vice President, or for Senator or Representative in Congress, shall not be denied or abridged by the United States or any State by reason of failure to pay any poll tax or other tax.

Section 2.

The Congress shall have power to enforce this article by appropriate legislation.

AMENDMENT XXV

Passed by Congress July 6, 1965. Ratified February 10, 1967.

Note: Article II, section 1, of the Constitution was affected by the 25th amendment.

Section 1.

In case of the removal of the President from office or of his death or resignation, the Vice President shall become President.

Section 2.

Whenever there is a vacancy in the office of the Vice President, the President shall nominate a Vice President who shall take office upon confirmation by a majority vote of both Houses of Congress.

Section 3.

Whenever the President transmits to the President pro tempore of the Senate and the Speaker of the House of Representatives his written declaration that he is unable to discharge the powers and duties of his office, and until he transmits to them a written declaration to the contrary, such powers and duties shall be discharged by the Vice President as Acting President.

Section 4.

Whenever the Vice President and a majority of either the principal officers of the executive departments or of such other body as Congress may by law provide, transmit to the President pro tempore of the Senate and the Speaker of the House of Representatives their written declaration that the President is unable to discharge the powers and duties of his office, the Vice President shall immediately assume the powers and duties of the office as Acting President.

Thereafter, when the President transmits to the President pro tempore of the Senate and the Speaker of the House of Representatives his written declaration that no inability exists, he shall resume the powers and duties of his office unless the Vice President and a majority of either the principal officers of the executive department or of such other body as Congress may by law provide, transmit within four days to the President pro tempore of the Senate and the Speaker of the House of Representatives their written declaration that the President is unable to discharge the powers and duties of his office. Thereupon Congress shall decide the issue, assembling within forty-eight hours for that purpose if not in session. If the Congress, within twenty-one days after receipt of the latter written declaration, or, if Congress is not in session, within twenty-one days after Congress is required to assemble, determines by two-thirds vote of both Houses that the President is unable to discharge the powers and duties of his office, the Vice President shall continue to discharge the same as Acting President; otherwise, the President shall resume the powers and duties of his office.

AMENDMENT XXVI

Passed by Congress March 23, 1971. Ratified July 1, 1971.

Note: Amendment 14, section 2, of the Constitution was modified by section 1 of the 26th amendment.

Section 1.
The right of citizens of the United States, who are eighteen years of age or older, to vote shall not be denied or abridged by the United States or by any State on account of age.

Section 2.
The Congress shall have power to enforce this article by appropriate legislation.

AMENDMENT XXVII

Originally proposed Sept. 25, 1789. Ratified May 7, 1992.

No law, varying the compensation for the services of the Senators and Representatives, shall take effect, until an election of Representatives shall have intervened

States' Rights Under the U.S. Constitution

Selective incorporation under the 14th Amendment

The U.S. Constitution has Articles and Amendments that established constitutional rights.

The provisions in the Bill of Rights (i.e., the first ten Amendments to the Constitution) were initially binding upon only the federal government.

In time, most of these provisions became binding upon the states through *selective incorporation* into the *due process clause* of the 14th Amendment (i.e., reverse incorporation).

When a provision is made binding on a state, a state can no longer restrict the rights guaranteed in that provision.

The 1st Amendment guarantees the freedoms of speech, press, religion, and assembly.

The 5th Amendment protects the right to grand jury proceedings in federal criminal cases.

The 6th Amendment guarantees a right to confront witnesses (i.e., Confrontation Clause).

The right to confront witnesses was not *selectively incorporated* into the due process clause of the 14th Amendment and is not binding upon the states.

Therefore, persons involved in state criminal proceedings as a defendant have no federal constitutional right to grand jury proceedings.

Whether an individual has a right to a grand jury becomes a question of state law.

The 10th Amendment, which is part of the Bill of Rights, was ratified on December 15, 1791. It states the Constitution's principle of **federalism** by providing that powers not granted to the **federal government** by the Constitution, nor prohibited to the **States**, are reserved to the States or the people.

Federalism in the United States

Federalism in the United States is the evolving relationship between **state governments** and the **federal government**.

The American government has evolved from a system of dual federalism to associative federalism.

In "Federalist No. 46," James Madison wrote that the states and national government "are in fact but different agents and trustees of the people, constituted with different powers."

Alexander Hamilton, in "Federalist No. 28," suggested that both levels of government would exercise authority to the citizens' benefit: "If their [the peoples'] rights are invaded by either, they can make use of the other as the instrument of redress."[3]

Because the states were preexisting political entities, the U.S. Constitution did not need to define or explain federalism in one section, but it often mentions the rights and responsibilities of state governments and state officials in relation to the federal government.

The federal government has certain *express powers* (also called ***enumerated powers***), which are powers spelled out in the Constitution, including the right to levy taxes, declare war, and regulate interstate and foreign commerce.

Also, the *Necessary and Proper Clause* gives the federal government the *implied power* to pass any law "necessary and proper" to execute its express powers.

Enumerated powers of the Federal Government are contained in Article I, Section 8 of the U.S. Constitution.

Other powers—the *reserved powers*—are reserved to the people or the states under the 10th Amendment. The Supreme Court decision significantly expanded the power delegated to the federal government in *McCulloch v. Maryland* (1819) and the 13th, 14th and 15th, Amendments to the Constitution following the **Civil War**.

Interpretation of the Constitution

Mode of Constitutional interpretation

There is disagreement over the analytical construct for interpreting the Constitution.

Living Constitution (closely aligned with Realism and Realist judges) changes to meet the needs of society.

> Mode 1: *legislative history* considers the intent during the enactment.

> Mode 2: *interpreting the text* has increased enormously as a mode of analysis.

>> Scalia: what I look for in the Constitution is what I look for in a statute: the *original meaning of the text*, not what the original draftsmen intended.

Ideological groupings

Ideology is a system of fundamental beliefs that specify appropriate and inappropriate conduct.

Judicial decisions often derive or, at least, align with the political ideology of judges, as has been empirically shown.

Conservatives on the court espouse a limited role for government in the private affairs of citizens, let markets rule.

Liberals on the court espouse an expanded role for the government in the private affairs of citizens.

Legal criticisms

Natural law is the unwritten body of universal moral principles underlying the ethical and legal norms by which human conduct is evaluated and governed.

Textualism is where judges have no authority to pursue broader social purposes or write new laws.

Strict constructionism was described by the late Justice Scalia as a degraded form of textualism.

Legislative intent looks for objectified intent as a reasonable person would gather from the text of the law placed alongside the remainder of the corpus juris;

>> the primary object of interpreting statutes is to ascertain the legislative intent *or* the meaning which the subject is authorized to understand the legislature intended; it is undemocratic to have the meaning of a law determined by what the lawgiver means rather than what the lawgiver promulgated. The intent of the lawgiver, not the judges.

Originalism (or *original intent*): what was meant by the drafters at the time it was written. Original meaning proposes what a reasonable person living when the language was ratified would believe the meaning.

Legal realism permits modification if furthering the function intended.

Living constitutionalism proposes that the Constitution must change.

Critical legal studies focus on race, gender, sex, weight, Marxism, and conflict.

The 4th and 5th Amendments Protections for Criminal Defendants

The Fourth Amendment to the U.S. Constitution protects persons and corporations from overzealous investigative activities by the government. It protects the rights of the people from unreasonable search and seizure by the government and permits people to be secure in their persons, houses, papers, and effects.

Reasonable searches are those (in most instances) predicated on a search warrant based on probable cause. Search warrants specifically state the *place and scope* of the authorized search. General searches beyond the specified area are forbidden.

Warrantless searches generally are permitted only 1) incident to arrest, 2) where evidence is in "plain view," or 3) where evidence likely will be destroyed. Evidence obtained from an unreasonable search and seizure is considered tainted and, under the exclusionary rule, is generally excluded from criminal prosecutions.

The Fifth Amendment provides that no person "shall be compelled in any criminal case to be a witness against himself." A person cannot be compelled to give testimony against himself or herself, although nontestimonial evidence, such as fingerprints and body fluids, may be required. This protection applies only to natural persons, not corporations and partnerships.

Based on Supreme Court decisions, it is improper for a jury to infer guilt from the defendant's exercise of their constitutional right to remain silent.

However, if the government wants to obtain evidence from one who has taken the Fifth, it can offer the person immunity, which means the government would agree not to prosecute the person based on the testimony they would give. The Fifth Amendment protects against double jeopardy, whereby a criminal defendant may not be tried twice for the same crime.

If the same criminal act involves several crimes, the accused may be tried for each crime without violating the double jeopardy clause. If the same act violates the laws of other jurisdictions, each jurisdiction may charge and try the accused.

Comprehensive Glossary of Legal Terms

Over 2,100 essential legal terms defined and explained. An excellent reference source for law students, practitioners, and readers seeking an understanding of legal vocabulary and its application.

Landmark U.S. Supreme Court Cases: Essential Summaries

Learn important constitutional cases that shaped American law. Understand how the evolving needs of society intersect with the U.S. Constitution. Summaries of seminal Supreme Court cases focused on legal issues, underlying principles, and judicial decisions.

Visit our Amazon store